THE OPERATIVE'S BLACK BOOK ON PERSONAL DEFENSE WITH FIREARMS

TABLE OF CONTENTS

Forward		4
About the author		5
Dedication		6
Acknowledgements		6
Warning/Disclaimer		7
Prologue		9

Section 1- Reflections of a Gunman 11

Chapter 1	The Mechanics of Defensive Shooting	13
Chapter 2	The Balanced Frame Of Mind	41
Chapter 3	Defensive Engagement and the Law	43

Section 2- The West Report on Defensive Shooting 45

Chapter 1	The Facts on Gun Control	45
Chapter 2	The Elements	51
Chapter 3	Actual Engagements	59
Chapter 4	Deadly Assault	67
Chapter 5	Methods for Survival	69

Section 3- The Stealth System of Personal Defense with Firearms 73

Chapter 1	A Superior System of Safety	74
Chapter 2	Threat Recognition	75
Chapter 3	The Hidden Threat	76
Chapter 4	Optimum Protective Capability	77
Chapter 5	Diversions	79
Chapter 6	Stealth Capability in Protracted Engagements	80
Chapter 7	Bullet Deflection	81
Chapter 8	Penetration Analysis	82
Chapter 9	Close Range Counter-Measures and Threat Neutralization	83
Chapter 10	Cover and Concealment	84
Chapter 11	Covering, Contamination, and Suppressive Fire	85
Chapter 12	Firepower	86
Chapter 13	The Controlled Shot	87
Chapter 14	The Protected Position	88
Chapter 15	Fire Zones and the Perimeter of the Crisis Point	89
Chapter 16	The Prepared State of Mind	90
Chapter 17	The Legalities	91

Section 4- Selecting Your Defensive Sidearm 93

Chapter 1	Making Your Selection	94
Chapter 2	The Merlin Seven Project	97
Chapter 3	Firearm Selection- Rifles, Carbines, and Shotguns	100
Epilogue		103

FOREWARD

Self-defense is a serious issue. How can you be expected to make the right decision if you are not fully informed?

The author presents some very interesting facts and anecdotes concerning handguns. Yes, handguns are dangerous, mainly to those who are uninformed and untrained in their proper use. This publication can make you more knowledgeable in handgun safety and how firearms should be used for your self-protection.

The founding fathers of this great country saw fit to write the Constitution to limit injustice, crime and tyranny, to "insure the domestic tranquility, provide for the common defense, promote the general welfare" for the people of the United States of America. Written in the Bill of Rights is their solution that "a well trained militia, being necessary to the security of a free State, the right of the people to keep and bear arms, shall not be infringed."

Many myths and untruths surround firearms. Institutions such as Handgun Control exploit fear and rely on exaggerations and misinformation to enforce their opinions that guns should be outlawed.

The National Rifle Association advocates for the publics free choice in firearms for personal protection and hunting. The NRA fully supports firearms training, practice and proficiency.

I support your personal choice to learn all you can about firearms and firearms safety. I agree with your choice to buy or not to buy a firearm. If you do buy a firearm, become proficient in its use and safety. Learn the hazards and benefits of carrying a weapon for self-protection. You must be fully aware and comply with the laws governing purchase and use of that firearm.

Make the choice that is best for you in respect to firearms and self-protection.

B.J. Keepers
U.S. Navy Seal Officer and
Law Enforcement Consultant

About The Author

As a bodyguard and security agent, he has provided protection for celebrities, politicians, executives, foreign dignitaries, and heads of State. He has been credited with saving several lives.

On courier operations, he has delivered millions of dollars safely.

As an investigator and operative he managed to stay alive while providing specialized information to clients that was occasionally obtained at considerable risk.

As a firearms instructor, he speaks with more than three hundred thousand rounds of experience. Those rounds went through hundreds of different firearms, including sub-machine guns. His former students include investigators, executives, notional defense specialists, security agents, and an Olympic shooter. This combined with his years of experience in carrying concealed weapons provides the reader with a very special insight.

This book and his book on home security will make life safer for those who read them. His personal defense and defensive firearms training courses are among the best in the industry.

If you are concerned about protecting yourself and your family with firearms, you're getting good solid information in this book from someone who knows first hand what it takes to stay alive when faced with mortal danger.

Randy S. Langley
Investigator

Operative 80 has years of experience, as a security agent, bodyguard, investigator, and international operative with what was the largest detective agency in the world and with other multi-national corporations.

He is currently self-employed as a security consultant and personal protection instructor.

Other publications authored by Operative 80 include: "The Operatives Black Book on Home Protection."

DEDICATION

This book is dedicated to my family, friends, and associates without whom this work would not be possible. And to the memory of Jane, who gave me a very special sense of security in this life.

ACKNOWLEDGEMENTS

Many thanks to the numerous firearms dealers who handle my publications; you provided the incentive for this book.

Special thanks to those who assisted with the research that helped make the production of this work possible. Law enforcement agents and officers, firearms instructors, and gun shop and range owners all helped contribute to this work.

Much of my tactical knowledge was derived from some of the most knowledgeable specialists in the business who ever lived. Some of them have passed on, but their life's work lives on.

People like Col. Rex, Applegate, Col, Jeff Cooper, FBI Tactician Robert Taubert, Major General Mitch Werbell, Ray Chapman, Paris Theodore, Chris McLoughlin and many others all made a positive difference in the world. If once in a great while I see a little farther, it is because I stood on their shoulders.

WARNING-DISCLAIMER

This book is sold as an educational aid for entertainment purposes. It is not all-inclusive and there may be omissions and errors, both typographical and in content within these pages. Further, I am not a lawyer, and those in need of legal advice should contact a qualified attorney.

There are certain inherent risks involved with any confrontation, and with regard to weapons handling and usage. The author and the publisher accept no responsibility for injuries or any other damages resulting from use of the information contained within this book.

The publisher and author ARE NOT advising or recommending that any individual purchase a firearm or other weapon for defensive purposes and ARE NOT recommending any person to engage themselves in any dangerous situation. That choice is left up to the individual's discretion and judgment.

Every effort has been made to provide information of a very high order within these pages. However, no warranty with regard to its effectiveness in any given situation is either expressed or implied by the author and publisher.

If you disagree with the foregoing statement, do not read this book. Give it to someone else who may benefit from the content and knowledge contained herein.

Over the years, I have provided enhanced peace of mind, safety, and security to countless individuals and I shall continue in the tradition of excellence to do so in the future.

Operative 80
Protective Specialist

THE OPERATIVE'S BLACK BOOK ON PERSONAL DEFENSE WITH FIREARMS

All rights reserved. No part of this book may be reproduced or transmitted in any form or by any means, electronic or mechanical, including photocopying, recording, or by any information storage or retrieval system without written permission from the author. Except for the inclusion of brief quotations in a review.

Copyright © 2014, Anthony B. Wojcicki
First Edition 2014
Printed in the United States of America

PROLOGUE

Over the years, a lot of information and misinformation has surfaced concerning the subject of defensive firearm's usage. Persons with limited knowledge and experience in this area often become bewildered and confused, or worse yet, formulate a system that could ultimately cost them their lives.

To compound the problem, several well-known individuals who are both knowledgeable and experienced in this matter, disagree on almost as many things as they agree upon. The result is often bad advice that can cost people their lives.

In this book, I will share with you my thoughts and the thoughts of others that have given me great comfort and capability in several very dangerous situations.

This will be accomplished in a simple and easy to understand fashion that will stay with you as it did with me. The words will be few, but the underlying principles can be the essence of a system that may someday save your life or the lives of others.

This text was developed especially for those who carry concealed weapons on a regular basis and for those who own firearms for defensive purposes.

It has only one purpose, that of making life safer for you and for others.

Operative 80
Northern Nevada
2014

SECTION 1

REFLECTIONS OF A GUNMAN

THE OPERATIVES PHILOSOPHY OF DEFENSIVE ENGAGEMENT

Always deter, de-escalate, evade, and/or avoid dangerous confrontations if possible. If you can't, and there is no way out, make good use of deception.

Don't allow the attacker(s) to surprise you.

You surprise him, her, or them.

Be the decisive winner in the engagement.

In this game, the loser sometimes takes a very hard fall.

Operative 80

THE MECHANICS OF DEFENSIVE SHOOTING

WEAPON SAFETY

Six rules to live by,
Memorize them.

1. Every gun is loaded until you have checked it and proven otherwise. Too many people have been killed by guns thought to be unloaded

2. Do not point a weapon at anything you don't want to destroy. Chances are good that you, the object, or the person you're pointing at will be destroyed.

3. Keep your finger off the trigger until you are ready to discharge the weapon.

4. Be certain of your target; what is behind the target; and the penetration capabilities of the weapon and cartridge you are using before you pull the trigger.

5. Know your weapon; learn its safe carry modes, its safety features, operating characteristics, capabilities, and limitations.

6. Wear ear and eye protection when on the shooting range.

FIREARMS AND MUNITIONS

As a rule of thumb, select the most powerful weapon that you can handle efficiently. If you live in an area where there is a range that rents handguns, go there and shoot a .22, a .38 using mid-range loads, a .38 Special using +P loads, .357 Magnum, and a .45 Auto.

If you find the .38 to be too intimidating and you are uncomfortable with it, don't go on to the .357 and .45. If you feel that you cannot handle the .38, purchase a reliable .22 and become very good with it.

Learn to make headshots out to 25 yards and you will probably do just fine if you ever have to. After you have learned to do it at 25 yards, practice doing it at 50 yards.

As a private citizen, it is unlikely that you will have to make distant shots in defense of your life, but it could happen.

There are some people who recommend modifying revolvers so that they can only be fired double-action. This, in my opinion, is a serious mistake. If you ever need to make a long range or precise shot, you will likely find it easier to accomplish in the single action mode. The factory put that capability there for a reason, and a very sound one at that.

If you live in a rural area where long-range defense is a possibility, you will want a rifle on hand. The Ruger Mini-14 Ranch Rifle is ideal for this purpose.

Yacht security calls for increased power and the Heckler and Koch 91 is, in my opinion, the gun of choice for the job. Place a few shots in a two to three foot area at the water line and you can sink a pirate's fiberglass vessel in short order.

Select a dark finish on your defensive firearms, preferably non-reflective. You do not want a gun that glows in the dark and gives away your position.

Consider wearing a second gun, the Model 638 Smith and Wesson, or a Smith and Wesson .22 kit gun combined with a second revolver or automatic with greater accuracy potential. Confrontations have occurred where those who have died might still be alive had they been armed with a second gun at the time of the encounter.

Those of you who are of small build will appreciate the small frame revolver and single column magazine automatic pistol. They will be easier for you to grip properly, and if your assailant is not stopped immediately, you will have fewer rounds to discharge to prevent the attacker from using your weapon on you.

Shoot your gun empty and toss it if you have to (unlikely if you are making headshots), but do not let the attacker gain possession of your gun.

I remember meeting a big man named John several years ago. He showed me the scars where he had been shot seven times with a 9mm Luger Handgun. None of the shots went into his head. He took one in the arm, one in the thigh, and five in his main body. He killed his attacker by choking him to death, after which he passed-out from blood loss.

John was alive, well, and driving a tractor-trailer when I last saw him. He was the 'good guy' in this confrontation, but had he been a 'bad guy', he almost certainly could have been stopped in this type of scenario with headshots.

A bullet in an attacker's brain is worth ten elsewhere when stopping an assailant is crucial.

Other incidents that come to mind include the story of the Deputy Sheriff who shot a would-be assailant in the foot with his .357 Magnum. The knife-bearing attacker shook his foot without any visible signs of discomfort to his foot. Compare this to an incident where an armed man was shot in the head with a .22 rim fire and dropped to the ground instantly, ceasing to be a threat.

Select a weapon that is comfortable for you and become good with it. Forget guns that you find difficult to control. A bullet that misses its intended target will not stop a determined attacker.

The most frightening noise in a gunfight is a snap audible from your weapon, when you wanted to hear a blast.

Check your ammunition, firearm, and firing pin therein regularly. Keep your weapon clean. Buy ammunition in case lots and shoot cartridges from several boxes randomly.

Make sure your cartridges have sealed primers.

Inspect all cartridges intended for defensive use before loading them.

Your weapon(s) and ammunition should be thought of as a unique life insurance policy, one that can keep you and yours alive. Buy the best available, take good care of them, and they will not let you down when you need them the most.

RECOMMENDED FIREARMS AND AMMUNITION

Handguns: .22 Caliber

1. Walther PPK/S .22
2. Colt Government Model and Rail Gun (Umarex) both in 22.
3. Ruger Standard
4. Smith and Wesson 22 Kit Gun and K-22

9mm Parabellum

1. Browning HI Power
2. SIG P-226 (Especially the Elite SAO)
3. Beretta 92 FS
4. CZ-75
5. Ruger P-95

38 Special

1. Smith and Wesson Model 638 Bodyguard (The original design)
2. Smith and Wesson Model 10

357 Magnum

1. Smith and Wesson Model 686
2. Ruger GP 100

357 SIG

1. SIG P-229

.40 S&W

1. H&K USP .40

45 ACP

1. Colt Government Model 1911
2. SIG Tactical Operations 1911
3. SIG Fastback 1911

Rifles

1. Ruger Mini 14 Tactical
2. Colt M4
3. SIG 716 Magpul

4. PTR 91

<u>Shotguns</u>

1. Mossberg 930 SPX
2. Remington 870

RECOMMENDED FIREARMS ACCESSORIES

1. Fist pocket and inside the waistband holsters made of Kydex
2. Galco Avenger Holster
3. Trijicon night sights and RMR and Reflex sights and scopes
4. EO Tech Holographic sight M-4 Colt
5. Speed Loaders for revolvers and extra magazines for autoloaders

RECOMMENDED AMMUNITION

1. .22 LR-CCI and Federal high velocity plated HP (hollow point) and solid.
2. 9mm Para. - Speed Gold Dot, Federal Hydra Shok, or Remington Golden Saber 124gr. JHP and Federal or Winchester 124gr. NATO Ammunition for hardened targets where extra penetration is needed.
3. 38 Special- Winchester 158gr. Lead Semi-Wadcutter Hollow Point +P (The old FBI Load) and Speer CCI Lawman 158gr. +P TMJ for enhanced penetration.
4. 357 Magnum- Winchester 145grain Silvertip JHP and Sellier and Bellot 158gr. FMJ for enhanced penetration.
5. 357 SIG- 125gr. Speer Gold Dot and Win 125gr. FMJ (for extra penetration where desired).
6. 40 S + W- Speer Gold Dot 165gr and Speer/CCI Lawman 165 TMJ (for extra penetration when needed).
7. 45 ACP- Federal Hydra Shok 230 Gr. JHP and 230 gr. FMJ for extra penetration
8. .223/5.56 mm- 50 to 55gr. JHP, and 55 FMJ and M-855 green tip penetrators (for hard targets)
9. .308/7.62mm- 147 to 150gr. NATO FMJ and Glaser and Factory soft points for reduced penetration
10. 12ga- Brenneke Slugs and 00 buckshot with Federal #6 game loads for reduced penetration in populated urban environment.

The Grip

Your grip on the handgun should position the web of your hand with the top of the grip frame and should be secure. A low thumb grip is more difficult for an assailant to break, and is thus superior in my opinion. When cocking a revolver into the single-action mode, do so with the thumb of your supporting hand using a two-hand hold for speed and accuracy.

Maintaining a constant grip is an asset in the accuracy department.

Stances and Holds

There are many shooting stances that have been developed over the years. I use the classic Weaver for shooting at distances greater than 7 yards. The classic gunfighters crouch makes sense up close when obstacles, concealment, or cover does not impair its use. I practice it regularly in conjunction with point shooting. Directing fire to your rear from this position can be accomplished with one hop when practiced to the point where it becomes natural.

The kneeling and prone positions have their place in shooting from behind cover and in certain long-range applications.

The squatting position has a lot of merit with a rifle.

Ideally, you should be able to shoot from any position that you may find yourself in. The only thing that really matters is the barrel's alignment with the target when the hammer falls, and that you are able to place accurate shots in any direction from where you are in time to save your life or the lives of others.

Shoot with the necessary degree of precision as rapidly as possible. Learn to shoot with either hand unsupported as well as with a two-hand hold. You never know when it might save your life after being wounded. When using a two-hand hold with a handgun, the fingers of the supporting hand should fit into the grooves between the fingers of the hand directly gripping the gun.

Shakespeare once said that, "He who hesitates is lost." Nowhere is this more true than in a gunfight.

The fastest draw is no draw, and a Smith and Wesson Model 638 in your jacket pocket with your hand on it can leave an armed assailant flat on his back in short order.

"Watch the hands" (of a potential assailant) was the advice given to me by a former U.S. Secret Service Agent while working with him on an assignment.

The best reload in a gunfight is no reload. Your firepower capability should be sufficient to cover any encounter that you may find yourself in. If you are using an automatic and are able to, reload while you still have one round in the chamber. An empty gun in a gunfight is bad news for the person holding it.

Where shooting is necessitated due to the violent actions of others, you want to be the one doing all or most of it.

I remember the advice of a New York Police Officer on gun fighting. He said, "Don't stop shooting until the armed assailant stops moving or ceases to be a threat."

The low thumb grip.

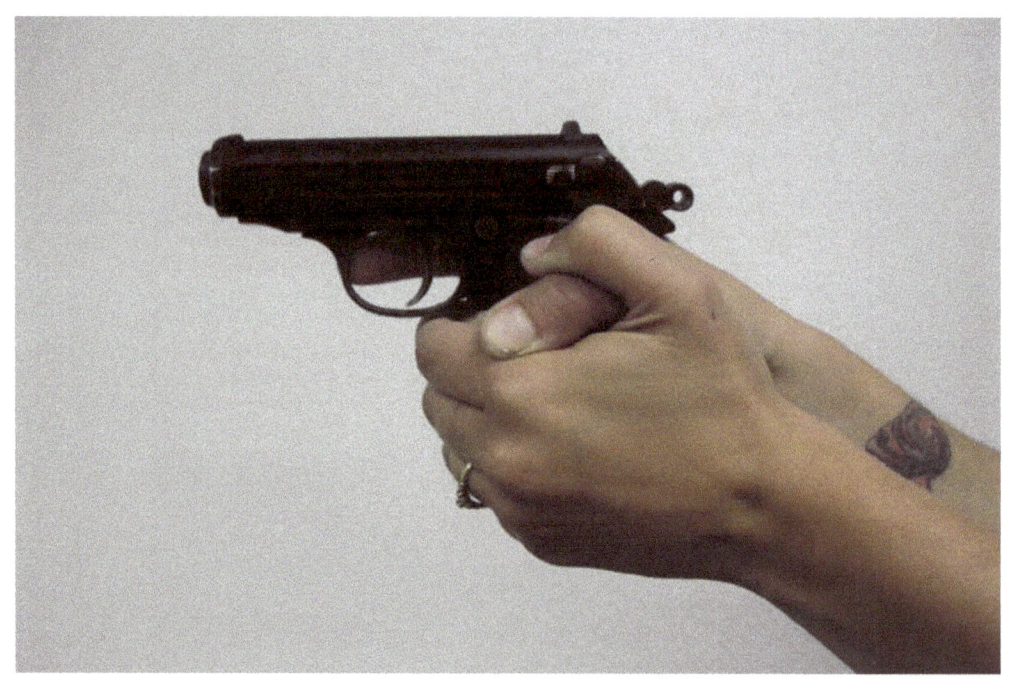

Two-hand low thumb grip and hold.

A different view of the two-hand low thumb-grip and hold.

Kimberly demonstrates the classic Weaver stance.

Kimberly demonstrates the kneeling position with a handgun.

Kimberly demonstrates the sitting position with a handgun. The position is similar with a rifle, but more angled.

Kimberly demonstrates prone with a handgun.

A different view.

Kimberly demonstrates the low ready position with a handgun.

Kimberly demonstrates point ready with a handguns only to be used when holding a dangerous threat at gunpoint.

Kimberly demonstrates the high ready position for use in crowded areas where low ready would result in inappropriate muzzle coverage of innocent persons.

Kimberly demonstrates the holster ready position, which is useful in giving a warning to a potential attacker. Note: This is not legal in all jurisdictions. In California it is considered brandishing once you break the plane going for the gun.

Kimberly demonstrates door/corner clearance methodology.

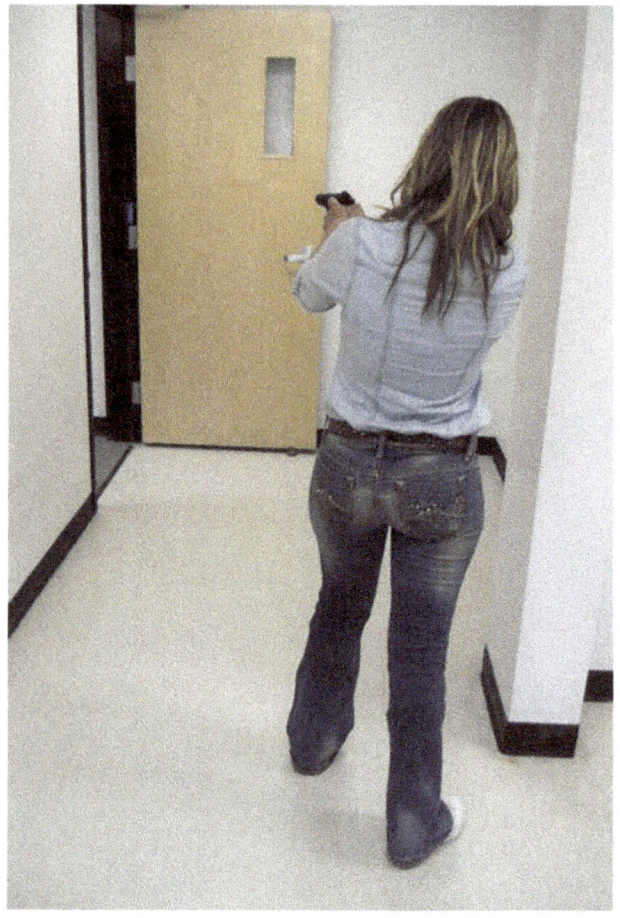

Kimberly demonstrates cover use. Not much of a target for the bad guy.

The low crouch position.

A different view of the low crouch.

Kimberly demonstrates the punch and shoot technique.

Fist is retracted to solar plexus following punch.

Kimberly demonstrates close range point shooting position with the tactical carbine. With muzzle lower and stock slightly higher, She would be in low ready.
Barrel pointed Up—high ready.
Raised to shoulder—point ready.

Off-hand with the tactical carbine.

Kimberly demonstrates the kneeling position with the tactical carbine.

Kimberly demonstrates the squatting position with the tactical carbine.

Kimberly demonstrates the prone position with tactical carbine.

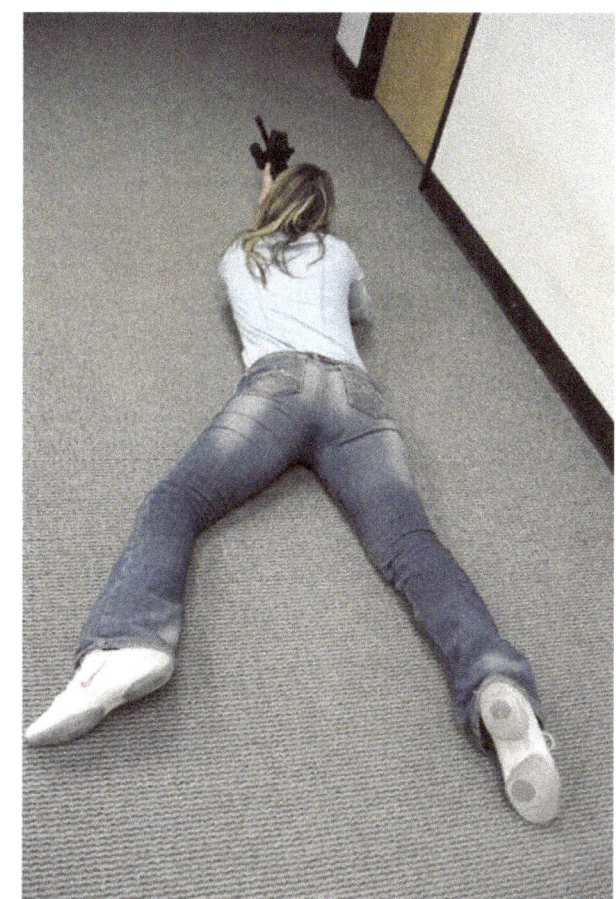

Another view of prone with rifle.

Kimberly demonstrates the bi-pod position with tactical rifle.

Another view of the bi-pod position with the Tactical Rifle.

There is the story that was told to me by an ex-FBI agent who was one of my instructors years ago, of the Federal Agent who was an exhibition shooter. He reportedly could hit multiple oranges in the air with his revolver consistently. One day after getting out of his car, he recognized a wanted felon. The felon simultaneously realized that he was in the presence of law enforcement and went for his gun. Twelve shots were fired that left both parties with empty guns and no hits on their respective intended targets. The agent wound up wrestling the felon into custody and vowed never to go out again without a reload. Oranges don't shoot back, but people sometimes do.

In the Old West there was a saying, "Beware of the man with one gun, he usually knows how to use it." Be even more aware of the man with two guns who knows how to use them. When fighting up close, always maintain as much distance between you and your assailant as possible; you don't want to be disarmed.

In a close-up gunfight, keep the weapon close to your side and take a step back with your foot under your gun hand. If your assailant is close enough, punch him in the nose and draw your fist to your chest while stepping back and discharging your weapon. This is known as the punch and shoot technique, and it can disorient the assailant enough to give you a clear edge in the fight.

At the onset of a gunfight, take cover if it is close and prudent to do so. If you are in a concealed position from a potential attacker, stay quiet and let him come to you.

Former Chief F.B.I Gunsmith Joe Varnich once gave an interesting explanation as to why he had cemented the eyes from a stuffed owl into the bottom of the Roper grips on his Colt Border Patrol Revolver. Colt's management gave the gun to him for being the creator of the design. His explanation: "I want to make sure I see what's behind me." Relevant thoughts when applied to gun fighting in today's world.

If a potential assailant enters an area such as your home and is unaware of your position, do not announce it. Maintain absolute silence and concealment with your weapon in hand. Keep the element of surprise on your side whenever possible. It may well be the last surprise the assailant will ever experience. Make sure it isn't your last surprise.

If you have to move to an area where obstacles, barriers, or corners of hallways or buildings are present, maintain a distance from them until they are checked and cleared of hostile targets. Your movement should be slow, deliberate, and at the greatest possible angle to afford you visual awareness of hostile targets hiding behind these types of areas. Ideally, stay back at least 7 yards from corners, barriers and obstacles when moving about them.

Never place yourself at the edge on an unchecked corner or against the wall adjacent to one. You never know who is at the invisible right angle, and bullets have been known to bounce off walls and into humans when fired at shallow angles. There is also the danger of being disarmed.

If your shoes announce your presence or movement, take them off. Loafers are obviously superior for this purpose and can be pushed off quietly with one's opposite foot.

If you are firing from behind cover, you will want to take a quick look from behind this area to determine the hostile targets location. Expose little more than one eye and your gun. Do not even expose this much of yourself at the same level twice in a row. Go high the first time, low the second and so on.

If you expose yourself to a hostile target from behind concealment, get the hell out of there fast using covering fire if you can't neutralize the attacker instantly.

Definitions:

Cover- material that will stop an assailants bullets
Concealment- Material that hides you from an assailant, but may not stop an assailants bullets
Covering fire- Shots fired at a hostile target in rapid succession to discourage gunfire on his part while you or someone else is moving to a different location

If you must go through a door without knowing what is behind it, shove or kick the door open if it opens into the area that you want to enter, while exposing as little of yourself as possible but still being able to see what is on the other side. Stay to the side adjacent to the door hinges as a rule. This will clear your immediate blind side with the door itself when the door opens into the area you want to enter, thus preventing instantaneous surprises from that area. Be ready to shoot the instant the door opens.

If the door opens outward, stay to the side opposite the hinges. Use a limited entry in either case, exposing as little of yourself as possible and then moving into the area quickly once you are sure of the blind spots and layout. If you do not have to enter an area like this, don't. It is extremely dangerous under the best of conditions.

Never accept an armed assailant's weapon handed to you as a gesture of surrender. Tell him or her to place it on the floor and step a minimum of ten feet away from it. An assailant, if knowledgeable, can turn a weapon on you in a split second, even if he or she is presenting the weapon butt forward and with the barrel pointed at his or herself.

If you have the opportunity to control lighting, do so in a manner that will illuminate the assailant and keep you in the dark. Special security companies have consoles that enable you to do this in your home. Avoid having light behind you if at all possible. If you can't, go into a position that poses the least possible silhouette to the attacker.

Several years ago, I investigated a shooting where a security agent was almost shot because he made the mistake of having a light on behind him in almost complete darkness. Do not make the same mistake; you may not be as lucky as he was.

As stated in the safety rules covered elsewhere in the text, be certain of your target before you discharge your weapon. A few years ago, a black belt karate expert shot his wife who had gotten up in the middle of the night to raid the refrigerator or whatever. He thought the noise was caused by an intruder in their home, and shot first without being sure of his target. Make sure that sort of tragedy does not happen to you.

Flashlights

Flashlights have improved greatly in the past few years. There are now aluminum bodied, police grade focused beam lights with the power to shoot a beam of light 400 yards, and can be purchased for well under $100 U.S. You can obtain a good one through renoconcealedweapons.com. Or, contact Tony the owner at 1-775-772-4508.

I prefer to use the old FBI Flashlight technique as it makes me a lesser target than other more modern methods. The old FBI method involves holding the light up, out, away, and slightly forward of your body so as not to illuminate you to an opponent. With the above-recommended light, you will blind your adversary in darkness.

Get the light where you want it, and positively identify the threat, then bring your gun on target and engage if necessary.

Establish fire zones within your home that minimize danger to other family members. With a little thought, you can arrange your home in such a manner that your family will be well protected while making things very tough for an intruder.

Muzzle Flash

Some firearms produce very little to no visible muzzle flash for their particular caliber (during night shooting), while others produce fireballs that significantly impair low light vision.

With few exceptions, the loads recommended in this book produce lower than average muzzle flash for their particular caliber.

None-the-less, you should practice shooting if at all possible under low lighting conditions so that you know what to expect and how your vision will be affected under such conditions.

Noise

Depending on the weapons used, a deafening effect may occur during the course of a gunfight. This is especially true with high-powered weapons when fired indoors. They are LOUD. Do not be startled by it, expect it.

When practicing at the range, shoot beside another shooter who is shooting a Magnum or beside the loudest weapon on the range. This will be disconcerting. Then envision that noise being created by the man-size target that you are firing at and shoot it to the best of your ability.

Body Armor

Body armor has saved a lot of lives since its invention. A good Level Two or Three vest is worthy of your consideration. If you elect to wear one, practice shooting while wearing it, these vests can be uncomfortable and may affect your mobility to a degree. But they will feel much better than a bullet in the chest.

Concealment

The Model 638 Smith and Wesson is most handy and effective when carried in a jacket pocket or a woman's shoulder bag with a special compartment for it. A good piece of cardboard covered with cloth will break up the guns outline in a pocket if placed between the gun and the outside of the jacket. With this system you can have your hand on the gun and fire through the pocket or bag if necessary. Nothing is faster.

With larger handguns, a good holster such as the Askins Avenger manufactured by Bianchi, or a good shoulder holster will serve you well. Whenever buying a holster, make sure you can get the gun out of it quickly in a sitting position. In a gunfight, you may be dealing with tenths of a second, and you want that gun of yours to come out of the holster like greased lightning.

Bullet Deflection

Where hard targets are concerned, a bullet tends to go straight when deflected at a shallow angle. To illustrate this, lets say an assailant is shooting at you from behind a car and you can only see his feet after he ducks behind the car for cover. By shooting at the pavement in front of his feet, odds are good that you will ricochet your bullets into the assailant.

Glass and metal when shot at tend to deflect the bullet at a greater angle. Learn to compensate for this. Example: An assailant shoots at you from inside a car and is behind a windshield that is angled upward. Shoot a little below where you want the bullet to impact, and your bullet will probably strike where you want. If you aimed at the assailant's forehead, the bullet might pass over their head entirely.

Barrier Penetration

Depending on the barrier hardness, thickness, angle involved with the caliber and bullet you are using, you may or may not be able to penetrate a barrier being used as cover by an armed assailant. If the armed assailant is behind a wall in your home, you know his location, the zone of your fire will not endanger innocent persons, and you are using a .45, .38, 9mm, or .357, shoot him through the wall.

Car bodies are about a 50/50 proposition with a .38 and .45 handgun ammunition; better with F.M.J 9mm, and .357 Magnum rounds. The less angle involved, the harder the bullet, and the more powerful the cartridge, the better your chances of penetrating the barrier.

Warning: F.M.J 9mm, .357, .223, .308 and numerous other loads and calibers that penetrate barriers well may penetrate excessively under different conditions and thereby endanger innocent human lives. Reserve this ammunition for use against hard targets or body armor where maximum penetration characteristics are desired. Remember Safety Rule #4- you are responsible for your actions.

Practice

The more you practice with a weapon, the better you will become with it. Vary your actual range practice as much as possible.

Close range shooting, from one to ten yards should constitute the majority of practice, with the remainder extending to fifty or even as far out as one hundred yards with a handgun. Practice with the rifle from two yards out to three hundred yards and incorporate below eye level (from the hip) shooting at close range.

Dry firing (firing the weapon without cartridges in it), will help you gain greater accuracy. Many knowledgeable persons suggest that you do this at the rate of ten dry fires for every live round expended. Snap caps are available from many gun shops that prevent damage to the weapon. Practice until you can dry fire the weapon with a dime balanced on the front sight without it falling off when the hammer falls. When you can do that, you will be able to hit what you want to.

Purchase a soft air handgun and practice drawing and firing with a large mirror in different light levels ranging from almost total darkness to too bright. Luminous paint will let you know where you are shooting in low light levels if applied to projectiles. Use your soft air gun against life-size targets or pictures that are partially obscured or concealed.

If you shoot enough, you and your gun will become as one. You will feel a burning sensation in your hand every time you hold it. Nothing is of greater comfort in times of extreme danger.

Deflecting an Attackers Weapon at Point Blank

If you ever find yourself under the attackers gun at spitting distance, deflect his or her weapon with your non-shooting hand by grasping the attacker's wrist and pushing it away from your body while simultaneously pivoting your body out of the line of fire and using your weapon on the assailant. This must be done at speed approaching or surpassing the speed of lightning to avoid being shot.

Multiple attackers

Several instructors include the *El Presidente* course in their defensive or combat firearms programs. I do not.

This course of fire requires four shots placed into each of three different targets, two shots at a time in forward and reverse sequence. In a reported actual shooting within the past few years, a person so instructed paid with his life. He fired two shots into the first armed attacker, and one into the second before the third shot him dead. The lone defender had time to fire three shots. Had he placed one in each of the hostile targets and then fired subsequent rounds at any who were still a threat, he might be alive.

Two shots fired in rapid succession are fine when you are dealing with a single assailant. They have the effect of increased stopping power and greater hit probability. This same philosophy, however, can get you killed fast if you apply it to multiple attackers.

For this same reason, I do not recommend match shooting as part of training practice. The courses of fire are often set up in such a manner that the shooter is forced to do things improperly… Things that in a real life shoot-out might get the defender killed.

THE BALANCED FRAME OF MIND

Not everyone reacts the same when faced with a dangerous confrontation. Many are shocked and surprised without the time for other emotions to develop. They sometimes die as a result.

On occasions where fear has time to enter one's mind-set, some will be paralyzed by it, others will convert the emotion to anger, and others will have their fight or flight instincts come into full effect. The tachy-psyche effect is part of this and it can and does occur instantly at the onset of a deadly confrontation in many people. I have experienced this myself and will describe its effect on my mental process below.

At the onset of my first life-or-death confrontation, an unknown person pulled a gun out of a paper bag at almost point-blank range, pointed it at me, and proceeded to cock the hammer of his .32 automatic pistol.

I was momentarily stunned (less than a quarter of a second). I remember thinking, *'Oh my God, I'm going to die,'* and then I felt a great calming effect come over me. Time seemed to move in very slow motion. My thinking and awareness became exceptionally clear. I remembered my training, deflected his weapon and drew mine, aiming it at his head. While deflecting his weapon, I managed to disarm him, and as a result I did not have to shoot him.

One witness, an experienced gunman himself, hit the floor from his chair at seeing my draw and remarked later, *'God damn, he drew that gun fast!'* This surprised me, for having been exposed to the tachy-psyche effect; the whole thing seemed to go by very slowly even though it was over in the time it takes to cock the hammer of a pistol.

Another interesting thing, after my assailant was disarmed and no longer posed a threat, I realized that the cylinder of my Smith and Wesson model 49 was partially rotated and the hammer was better than halfway back in the double action mode. I released the trigger which moved forward perhaps a quarter of an inch.

Ironically, I had no recollection of having applied any trigger pressure at all, yet my assailant came very close to death. Had I been holding a single action automatic pistol that day, I have no doubt that I would have shot him, and I would have been legally justified in doing so.

An old friend named Jimmy had a couple of interesting philosophies concerning the mental process when facing danger. The first I believe to be his own, the second is borrowed from Shakespeare.

Jimmy said, "In most cases, the person who makes up his mind as to what he is going to do, and does it quickly, and without reservation is the one who will be the winner in that situation." Then he added, "A coward dies a thousand deaths, a brave man only one. I cannot understand why men will fear, when death, a natural thing must surely come."-Shakespeare.

Then there are the words of former Olympic Shooter, Michael Thompson who said, "If you think you can or you can't, you're probably right."

An F.B.I. certified firearms instructor who has survived six gunfights had these thoughts, "Your odds of surviving a gunfight are better than 50/50. Your odds of surviving if you get shot are about 50/50. If you take a hit, keep shooting, you may not survive but perhaps you will end your attackers career and prevent another innocent person from being shot." Yes, he has been shot, but you would never know it, seeing him in action.

"Anything can happen to anybody, anytime." Langley's Law, courtesy of Randy S. Langley, Investigator (and a fine one at that).

"If it doesn't look right, it probably isn't." Operative 80's Law. Get away from it if you can. No matter how good you are there is always the chance that you will be the loser in a violent confrontation. You are better off to avoid it if at all possible.

Those who can see and/or sense the invisible can sometimes do what would otherwise seem impossible. Expect the unexpected and pay close attention to your sixth sense.

"You pull the trigger, and the rest is up to God." –Ed Beach, former Pinkerton Investigator, while on assignment.

DEFENSIVE ENGAGEMENT AND THE LAW

Know the law in your state and the prevailing mood of the courts. Know when you can and cannot shoot legally.

Have the phone number of a fighting attorney with a good track record in self-defense cases in your wallet and in a separate location at home or left with your most trusted friend or family member. You may be allowed only one phone call if arrested in the aftermath of a shooting. Make sure it counts.

Take a State or Federally mandated certified firearms training course if possible in your area. Save all documentation.

Do not hesitate to enlist the services of an expert witness such as Massad Ayoob or myself if you are charged in a shooting.

Politely invoke your Fifth Amendment rights if involved in a shooting. Explain to the police that you would prefer to speak with a lawyer prior to any questioning.

Always remember, your intent and objective in a defensive encounter is only to stop the attacker from harming you or others.

You will normally be asked if you intended to kill the person by the police, and if you answer that question with 'yes', you may well have bought a first degree murder charge. Your reply, if you reply at all, should be, "No, I had to stop him from killing me or someone else", whichever is applicable. This implies that you feared for human life when you acted, which is a requirement in some states.

Understand the concept of disparity of force. A jury in most instances will not conclude that your actions were reasonable if you shoot an unarmed seven year old. However, if you were a frail old lady whose home was invaded by a six-foot thug who lunged at you violently, most jurors would conclude that your actions were reasonable if you shot him.

In most, if not all cases, a private citizen must fear for his or her life or the life of another, and have a valid reason before deadly force can be used as a means of defense.

Some states have laws that require you to take an avenue of escape if there is one available to you. This is just good common sense whether it is the law in your area or not. In any confrontation, there is always the chance, however slim, that you will be the loser. Always avoid one if you can.

I remember the response of a former Judge and State Assemblyman upon being told of my defensive actions in the confrontation where I disarmed the individual without having to shoot him. Bear in mind that the Judge regularly carried a Cold Diamondback revolver or two for defensive purposes.

His nickname for me was "Rasputin" (apparently he thought I was difficult to kill).
The Judge approached, with a steely-eyed look and said, "Rasputin, one of these days that trigger finger of yours if going to get you into trouble."

I replied, "Well Judge, what would you have done if someone pulled a gun on you?"

The Judge gave me a crooked smile, and approving look, and said, "Hell, I'd have shot him."

Sherriff Ottie J. Moore once said "Put yourself on the jury, before you pull the trigger."

Keep in mind of course, that, "It is better to be tried by twelve, than carried by six." –Originator Unknown.

Some years ago, one of the most prolific firearms' instructors in the world was asked about mastering personal defense with a sidearm. He replied to the effect that when one could survive a surprise attempt upon his life and be more dangerous to his attacker than the attacker was to him, that he had mastered such defensive engagement.

As one who has met the foregoing criteria along with others whose thoughts appear in this work, I sincerely hope you never have the need to.

SECTION 2

THE WEST REPORT ON DEFENSIVE SHOOTING

"There are only two things that guarantee the continued freedom of the American people: Freedom of Expression and the Right to Keep and Bear Arms."

Larry King
A former crocodile hunter from Australia.

The Facts About Gun Control

Years ago I read an ad, paid for by Handgun Control Inc., which featured Sarah Brady and the President of the Fraternal Order of Police, whose membership includes some of the nations police officers.

The ad had "MACHINE-GUNS, COP KILLER BULLETS, and PLASTIC PISTOLS" in bold print. The president of the Fraternal Order of Police asks the question, "has the N.R.A. gone off the deep end?" The ad is continually anti-gun.

Having spent ten years as an investigator at the highest levels in our society, I decided to investigate the facts. By the way, I was not an N.R.A. member at the time. I have since joined and recommend that you do as well if you wish to preserve firearms rights.

The following F.B.I. statistics are most enlightening.

In 1986, a crime was committed every two seconds. Two hundred and sixteen million, three hundred and thirty-two thousand crimes were reported committed in 1986, almost one for every man, woman, and child in America.

In 1986, a violent crime was committed every 21 seconds in the United States.

The F.B.I. estimates that 20,613 persons were murdered, about 40% with handguns, 60% by other means, one every 25 minutes.

90,434 reported victims were raped, one every six minutes. A handgun in the hands of a trained and skilled person might have prevented any one of them.

834,822 persons were victims of assault, one every 38 seconds. About 20% of aggravated assaults involved firearms, more assaults were committed with knives.

542,775 persons were robbed, one every 58 seconds. 34% involved firearms, 66% did not.

3,241,410 American homes were burglarized—was your home one of them? One in three American homes will be touched by crime this year.

By contrast, 65 police officers were killed in the line of duty. 20 of those died in domestic disputes and according to another source 25% of the officers were killed with their own gun.

Back when I went to school to become an investigator, a police instructor told me that statistically, the average police officer is on the scene to stop a major crime in progress once every 14 years. Crime has increased since that time.

So where are the police when all of these crimes are being committed? They are on the job, off-duty, on break, writing traffic violations, or in court. They are overworked in many instances and subject to public pressure.

Criminals are not stupid to the point where they knowingly strike in the presence of the police.

The statistics on crime conclusively prove that the police cannot always protect you, as much as they would like to.

You have to be able to protect yourself, and if a handgun were not the best tool for the job, the police would not be using them.

In my research material, I have four pictures of zip guns made by criminals out of pipe. They were all tested and they all work. They are the property of the Los Angeles Police Crime Lab, and there are undoubtedly more in existence.

A federal agent requested that I witness and appraise the value of six submachine guns that were manufactured illegally in Florida. The agent purchased these guns for $600.00 each before making the arrest. The agent said of the guns, "They work very well."

In the San Francisco Bay Area, three police officers were found in the possession of illegal machine-guns. The guns were stolen from a military arsenal. A police officer was charged with the theft after reselling the weapons to other officers who purchased them illegally.

Senator Edward Kennedy's bodyguard was arrested in Washington D.C. for illegally carrying sub-machineguns. I'm sure the senator voted to outlaw the manufacturing of them. I suspect that he feels safer knowing that he is one of the few people who have that level of protection. He did not seem to care whether you are well protected or not.

In Lake Tahoe, a security officer shot an armed robber with his handgun in a casino. The armed robber was shooting up the casino with his weapon. Unfortunately, the robber was wearing a bulletproof vest. Police officers outside the casino were finally able to stop the felon by shooting him in the leg. It appears that the security and police officers could have used some of those COP KILLER BULLETS, and if that criminal's target had been your home instead of the casino, so could you. Under the new law, private citizens and security officers cannot own them. At least one casino is teaching their people to shoot for the head according to my sources.

The plastic pistol and terrorism? They had better worry more about the plastic bomb. It is a lot more dangerous and has already been used to destroy jetliners.

We live in a land where criminals make homemade guns, bombs, and hand grenades. If you do not believe that about the hand grenade, just ask the Florida police officers who were injured in the blast when trying to apprehend the criminal who had one.

Yet, the anti-gun people tell us that armed American citizens are undermining the civilized response to crime.

Take the case of the farm family of six who were murdered by escaped convicts. The five men were executed one by one. The 26 year-old woman was taken to the woods, raped, and then executed. They were very civilized; they did not use a gun to defend themselves against this tragedy.

In Kennesaw, Georgia, a law was passed that required gun ownership in every household. The result showed an 86% reduction in violent crime and burglaries for the first year.

In Miami, Florida, I'm told by sources that violent crime has been cut in half since passage of the gun law in Florida that permits citizens of good character to carry concealed weapons.

In New York City, they have a very restrictive gun law. It is tough for the average citizen to own one legally. Crime is rampant, and when an honest citizen who has been hospitalized as the victim of a mugging stands up and fights back against three thugs, it frightens the criminals in the city. These criminals consider it their God given right to rape, rob, and murder innocent victims. And when somebody like Bernie Geotz shoots them in self-defense, they become paranoid. The result is a 50% reduction in violent crime on New York streets following the Geotz shooting.

Bernie Geotz did more to prevent and reduce crime in one minute with a few bullets than the New York Police Department did all year.

They thanked him, by sentencing him to six months in jail for illegally carrying the means by which he legally defended himself. He appealed the case, of course.

I guess it just is not safe for criminals to roam the streets with people like Bernie Geotz on the loose… and the word gets around…

If you were to take a pistol and put it in front of you, you might realize two things:

In the hands of another person, that gun or any other functioning weapon can be used to control your behavior or kill you.

That same gun in your hands can preserve your freedom and may one day save your life.

There are only two things that guarantee the freedom of the American people: freedom of expression and the right to keep and bear arms.

On the day that we lose those rights, America as a nation governed for and by the people will be a thing of the past.

Let us preserve the freedom with the largest armed populace in the free world.

GUN CONTROL

First supporters: Joseph Stalin and Adolph Hitler

Hitler's thoughts on the subject: "There you stand with your law, and here I stand with my gun. Which one do you think will prevail?"

58% of Americans who own handguns, own them for protection. 14% of Americans have used them for self-defense.

650,000 law-abiding citizens successfully defend themselves with a handgun against criminals each year. 300,000 use long guns for protection each year. Statistically, 1,781 people successfully defend themselves with handguns everyday in America. (According to Criminal Justice Department at Florida State University, released by Dr. Gary Kleck).

THE FIRST SHOOTING BY A CCW HOLDER IN FLORIDA

Cab driver Mark Steven Yuhr, described by neighbors as a solid citizen and not a 'Rambo-type', was in the process of being robbed at gunpoint. He drew his lawfully concealed .45 automatic handgun and shot the robber, identified by police as Orlando Hernandez Barroso. Barroso was pronounced dead at Jackson Memorial. Mr. Yuhr's wallet was found in his pocket.

Barroso was described as having a long criminal record, and a history of trying to kill police officers. Police Sergeant Gerald Green said upon investigating the shooting, "This sends a major message to the robbers."

The U.S. Justice Department tells us that armed citizens kill two to three times more criminals than the police every year. Their study of 1,800 prisoners serving time showed that:
- 60% feared being shot by an armed citizen more than being shot by the police

- 53% did not commit a specific crime for fear of being shot by the victim.
- The armed citizen is possibly the most effective crime deterrent in the nation
- A 26-city survey of 32,000 attempted rapes reveals that 32% were actually committed, but only 3% of attempts were successful against women defending themselves with knives or guns.

The F.B.I. has statistics that show that the robbery rate in the 11 states with concealed weapon carry provisions is less than half the rate in the rest of the United States in 1986.

THE WAITING PERIOD

1975, Washington D.C.- two men break into a house shared by three women. The police are called but take no protective action. The three women are repeatedly raped and beaten for the next 14 hours. The women sued the Police Department and lost on the grounds that the Police are not obligated to protect any individual, only the public at large.

1981, Dade County, Florida- Police received 700,000 calls for help. They responded to 200,000 of them. A half-million calls unanswered. When asked why everybody in Dade County goes out and buys a gun, Attorney General Smith replied, "They damn well better; they've got to protect themselves."

In San Leandro, California, a single mother was forced to endure 15 days of terror at the hands of her maniacal neighbor due to the waiting period. She killed her attacker the day after she picked up her gun.

The 911 terrorists did not use a handgun for murder; they were not affected by a waiting period. I wonder if any of the victims they murdered were?

New York has one of the strictest gun laws in the country, and three times the violent crime of Virginia which has no waiting period and is often criticized by gun control advocates as having lax gun laws.

In Gary, Indiana, the mayor ordered his police chief to refuse to provide applications to citizens that were required to purchase a handgun. Do you want this to happen where you live?

According to *U.S. News and World Report,* for every 100 police officers on duty at any given time, 45 are on patrol, and they spend 15% of their time dealing with violent crime.

Decision Making, Inc. conducted a poll in 1978—the result was that citizens were against a waiting period by a margin of 2-1.

The U.S. Senate rejected a waiting period by a 3-1 margin.

84% of police chiefs surveyed said they believed their own inability to protect citizens at all times was sufficient reason to have an armed American citizenry. (According to the Executive Director of the National Association of Police Chiefs). He added, "You are more likely to find a police officer when you run a red light than when you need one in a violent situation."

Federal Aviation Administration representatives testified before the U.S. House committee that they are aware of no non-metallic firearm that is not reasonably detectable by present technology and methods in use at our airports today.

The initial so-called 'armor-piercing ammunition' legislation would have outlawed almost all-hunting ammunition.

Not once has a legally owned and registered fully automatic weapon been used in the commission of a crime.

Priscilla Ford was on death row in Nevada for deliberately murdering 7 people with her automobile. A 4,000-pound vehicle at speed makes a .44 Magnum look like a sneeze by comparison. We would save a lot more lives if we banned cars instead of handguns, but I do not see Sarah Brady backing such legislation.

In more recent times, the liberals in Congress and State Legislatures have sought to create gun free zones. At Virginia Tech, the Aurora Movie Theater, and Sandy Hook Elementary school, criminals ignored the law and there were no armed defenders present as a result of the gun free zone laws.

Even military personnel were left unarmed at Fort Hood and the Washington Navy Yard shootings.

As Wayne La Pierre of the NRA implied, "Good guys with guns stop bad guys with guns." It has been proven for more than 100 years.

When you look at the big picture and not just a few isolated incidents, you realize the correct approach to gun control is that of being able to deliver accurate fire in defense of life… perhaps yours.

THE ELEMENTS

"If you have a choice between being lucky or being smart, pick lucky every time."

-A retired Marine in California who likes his guns
the way he likes his women: "short, black and hot."

There are, in my estimation, some thirty basic elements that are invariably the determining factors in armed engagements. Any one of them can mean the difference between life and death for any party involved in the engagement.

They are not collectively involved in every engagement, but there is a potential of any of them being present in any given armed action.

Seven of these elements are physical in scope, nine are mechanical, and the remaining elements are intangible.

Let us look at them by group and individually.

THE PHYSICAL ELEMENTS

1. Speed into action—the ability to deliver the first shot in the encounter.

    This has been a major factor in the outcome of many gunfights, and those who were victorious were not always the ones who fired first.

    Bullets that hit dirt or fly over an opponents' head may not solve the immediate problem at hand, which brings us to the second physical element.

2. The ability to deliver accurate gunfire to the target.

    Sometimes the fellow who shoots a little slower and hits his mark is the victor over the fast draw artist who misses.

    In any event, the ability to deliver accurate fire cannot be overemphasized.

3. Conclusive power—the power or force that concludes the action

    This may or may not involve guns or bullets. I know of a man who choked his attacker to death after being shot seven times with a 9mm handgun at close range.

    It may involve a gun, but as we will see later in other examples, the outcome of an armed engagement may be decided by power generated by something other than gunpowder.

4. The detection capabilities of the individuals involved at the onset of, or prior to the action.

The individual who detects trouble in advance and who takes the initiative to preserve his survival may be miles ahead of the game.

Remember West's Law: "If it doesn't look right, it probably isn't."

5. Defensive movement

The average man still shoots high, bullets still do not penetrate hard cover, and a handgun that has been deflected prior to ignition will not deliver accurate fire to the initial target. These are relevant thoughts when faced with an armed encounter.

6. The ability to employ stealth efficiently

In situations where stealth is relevant to the action, it can be the single greatest determining factor.

The ability to move quietly, remain invisible to an opponent, avoid bumping into the wrong person in darkness, and the lack of a strong after-shave or perfume can, in reality, mean the difference between life and death.

7. Mental capabilities

The ability (or lack of it) to function under stress and control one's emotions will in many instances affect the outcome of an armed action.

The fellow who has such ability, otherwise referred to as 'nerves of steel', may have a decisive advantage.

The preceding seven elements, which the individual may or many not have control over, are physical in scope. Those who can exercise control and execute the right moves have a head start on victory in an armed action.

THE MECHANICAL ELEMENTS

8. Weapon reliability

A gun that goes 'bang' every time is a definite advantage in a gunfight. A gun that goes 'snap' is an absolute liability that can cost you your life.

Have you ever wondered why Smith and Wesson and Colt revolvers with direct ignition dominated the police and security markets for so many years? Now you know!

9. Weapon durability

Over the years, there have been a number of trigger guards bent over an opponent's head. This can and does put them out of commission.

Fighting can be rigorous, and it pays to have a durable weapon that will stand up to the rigors of combat. There might be a second armed opponent after a physical blow was delivered to subdue the first.

Anything can happen in a gunfight and it pays to have a strong gun.

10. The intrinsic accuracy of the weapon

    An excellent shooter with a gun that delivers mediocre accuracy is in increasing trouble as the range of the gunfight is extended; whereas, the same shooter with an accurate gun has an added advantage.

    In a gunfight, you cannot have too much advantage

11. Stopping and penetrating power

    A bullet/cartridge combination with a good stopping power record is always a plus.

    A bullet/cartridge combination with an enhanced penetration capability can be an asset or a liability. Fortunately, designs exist which perform the desired functions rather well.

    A bullet that penetrates the intended target and endangers innocent persons behind that target is a liability in such situations.

    Conversely, this same type of bullet may be required if the intended target is behind a barrier, and, as such it is nice to have a few rounds on hand for such scenarios.

    Oh yes, these things do make a difference in who walks away and who rides to the hospital or coroners office. A bullet that fails to stop its intended target can have permanent results for the person who fired it.

12. Weapon controllability

    A highly controllable weapon affords the user an important advantage, whereas, one with severe recoil impulse (kick) impedes the shooter's ability.

    A weapon that produces a fireball for muzzle flash may seriously damage the shooters chances for survival in a nighttime engagement.

    A weapon that deafens the shooter may have fatal repercussions for its user.

    How much of a factor can this be in the outcome of a gunfight? —If a second shot is needed by the shooter, a big one!

13. Firepower capability of the weapon

   People die in gunfights because they run out of bullets—people like police officers and F.B.I. agents.

   Some old-time peace officers may have felt that six shots were enough, but not the better ones.

   Doc Holiday carried two revolvers and so did a lot of other gunfighters of his day.

   An empty gun in a gunfight is bad news for the person holding it.

   How much is enough?

   As much as possible!

   If you do not believe me, just ask the Egyptian security people who were there when Sadat was assassinated.

14. Stealth capability of the weapon

   Stainless steel guns are all the rage these days, and nickel plated guns have their share of followers as well. Statistics show that more than 80% of shootings occur at night. What better way of advertising your position than by having a nickel-plated or stainless steel gun? They will stand out like a neon sign saying, 'here I am, shoot me!'

   One of the well-known gun writers once suggested racking the slide of a pump shotgun as a deterrent to intruders in the home.

   I recently overheard another fellow who fancies himself as a combat shooter commenting on the virtues of racking the slide of a shotgun or automatic pistol at the onset of defensive action to intimidate opponents. Of course the most dangerous targets that he has engaged were bowling pins in a shooting match.

   The fact of the mater is that any signal, visual or audible, is likely to draw fire from an armed adversary.

   If you ever find yourself beside me in a dark place defending your life and mine against an armed aggression, you will not hear noise from the cocking mechanism of an H&K P-7 or movement from the slide of a shotgun. The only sound you will hear coming from my practically invisible parkerized Colt or Browning will be the ignition of gunpowder.

15. Pointing characteristics of the weapon

A gun that points well for the shooter can make all the difference in a nighttime defensive action. You may not be able to see the sights or the adversary and yet you may know the adversaries general location from the muzzle flash of his weapon.

16. Speed at which the weapon can be deployed
    A gun that takes one second to get into action can cost the owner his or her life.

    People have died in gunfights because they were a fraction of a second slower in getting off that crucial shot that might have been able to save their lives.

    The faster the gun is on target, the better when it comes to gun fighting. As Shakespeare once said, "He who hesitates is lost."

The nine preceding elements are the mechanical elements of gun fighting. They all pertain to the gun and any one of them can result in fatality, yours or someone else's.

THE INTANGIBLE ELEMENTS

17. Tactical knowledge and judgment

    If there is time for these elements to come into play in an armed action, the one who has these elements working in his favor has a tactical edge in the encounter. The selection of method and manner of action has much to do with the outcome of a gunfight.

18. Use of cover (material that will stop a bullet)

    Cover saves lives—a lot of them. If it is close by, it beats the hell out of standing in the open in a gunfight.

    It does affect the outcome of shooting incidents. Just ask the New York Police Department; they win the vast majority of them with the use of cover.

    Body armor is some of the best cover available, if you are wearing it when the bullets start flying. It has saved countless lives.

19. Use of stealth

    Where this element is brought into play, it is all but conclusive in action. The advantages of having stealth working in your favor may well be impossible for the opponent to overcome. How many terrorist ambushes have you heard of that were unsuccessful? This tactic works for both sides, you know. The only thing more decisive in a gunfight than an ambush is a counter-ambush.

Stealth is a major factor in the outcome of gunfights. John Westley Hardin would vouch for that, if he were alive. He was killed as a direct result of stealth. Many credit him as the greatest gunfighter of all time.

Makes you think, doesn't it?

20. Use of deflection

    The use of deflection, whether it is that of your opponents weapon or that of your bullets bouncing off a hard surface into your adversary, can determine the outcome of an armed action.

    A little girl was shot and killed by a drug dealer in Florida. The bullet bounced off the wall in her house. Too bad that a similar bullet couldn't have bounced off the pavement into the dealer prior to his firing of the fatal shot that killed the child.

    Deflection of the opponents weapon at spitting distance can prevent bullet holes in flesh—maybe yours.

21. Use of lighting

    In a nightmare encounter, those who control lighting to their advantage in an intelligent fashion, have distinctly better odds of surviving the action.

    Those who use light foolishly under such circumstances aren't apt to be around long enough to regret it.

22. Use of terrain

    If an opponent's path can be intelligently channeled during an armed encounter, that opponent is at a distinct disadvantage.

    For centuries, men have known that the man on higher ground has an advantage. Not always, but usually.

    If an intruder enters your home and must pass up a staircase to get to you, and you use the top of that staircase for cover until the assailant makes his move up the stairs and open fire, the assailant is in deep trouble. You have cover and as a result of the terrain the intruder has no such luxury.

23. The range of the engagement and accuracy capability thereto

    The distance involved can have a lot to do with the outcome of an engagement.

    The accuracy capability of the shooters is a factor here, as is the accuracy of the weapon and the trajectory of the cartridge it shoots.

A man armed with a handgun in the open is at a distinct disadvantage if he is facing a man with a rifle who is behind cover 150 yards away.

24. Outside intervention

    You can have an opponent dead to rights, but if he has an accomplice who sneaks up behind you and delivers the first blow, the situation can change dramatically.

    If outside intervention is to occur in an armed action, it is best to have it working on your behalf.

25. Possible disengagement by an assailant

    This changes everything, and it is all to the better. It happens surprisingly often.

    If an opponent decides to disengage, let him, unless he has done something like committing murder in your presence.

26. The number of individuals involved and the tactical order of engagement

    The number of individuals involved in an armed battle can be a formidable factor in determining the outcome, as can the manner in which they were engaged.

    Five or more armed men against one man armed with a pistol are lousy odds if you happen to be the one man; but Sergeant York proved in World War 1 that it could be done under the right circumstances.

27. Diversions or warning noises

    A man who is awakened by an alarm, broken glass, or the barking of a dog and reflexively arms himself, stands a much better chance of survival against a murder attempt than one who remains asleep.

    Conversely, the burglar who makes noise coming up the stairs in the dark has just identified his position.

    The burglar who shoots in darkness at the noise made by a dirty penny thrown as a diversion has just identified his position by the signal emitted by his muzzle flash. His chances of surviving the encounter have diminished accordingly.

28. The will to live

    Some people fall down and die when they are shot, others keep shooting.

    The will to live can be a major determining factor in an armed confrontation.

29. The metabolic state of those involved

   Alcohol, drugs and adrenaline can all be factors in the outcome of a gunfight. If an individual does not feel pain, he does not know he has been shot and may not be affected in terms of his ability to kill.

   In addition, reflexive action and electrical impulse can trigger return fire from an assailant at the moment of death.

   Let the shooter beware!

30. Luck

   Just plain, 'dumb luck'.

   There is another fellow who has written a book on defensive shooting and gun fighting in general.

   In this book, he advises the shooter to shoot for the belt buckle of an opponent at close range. A couple of years ago I read about a shooting in a newspaper in San Francisco.

   The fellow was shot in the belt buckle and the belt buckle stopped the bullet. He was for all practical purposes unscathed.

   YOU CAN'T BEAT LUCK…

ACTUAL ENGAGEMENTS

"WRAP, LOCK AND PRAY."
(Wrap your hands around the grip, lock onto the target, and pray for survival.)

Ed Rieg
N.R.A. Certified Police Instructor
Rieg's Gun and Range
Orlando, Florida

Statistics compiled from three different reputable sources integrated together indicate the following:

GUNFIGHT STATISTICS

Distance—7 yards or less
Number of shots fired—fewer than 5 from all parties involved
Time span—less than 3 seconds
Accuracy—average person shoots high
Time frame—80%+ occurred at night
Police officers shot with own weapon—about 25%
Accuracy by Police—25% hit probability with any given shot in actual gunfire

TRENDS

A considerable number involve multiple threats.
Increased distance somewhat more common.
High-capacity 9mm pistols more commonly in use.

The preceding statistics represent averages. Gunfights are anything but average and if you happen to find yourself in one that is not average, those statistics will not mean much to you.

Consider the following examples:

1. Hostage Rescue:

    An officer covertly places himself behind the hostage taker and fires a 9mm safety slug. The hostage taker's eyes went into the woman's hair as the slug impacted. The hostage was physically unharmed due to stealth and the specialized ammunition.

2. Florida Officer in the bar:

    The officer had his man (a dangerous felon) at gunpoint. Though he wanted to look behind him, he could not afford to take his eyes off the man he had at gunpoint for an instant. Unknown to the officer, an accomplice had positioned himself behind the officer with a club ready to swing at the officer's head. Fortunately, a back-up officer entered the establishment just prior to the swing and ordered the accomplice to drop the club. Had he entered one second later, the officer initially making the arrest would have been on the floor.

3. The Bodyguard at the nightclub:

    After the director of an exclusive private membership nightclub in northern California placed a woman in a cab at her request, the Frenchman who had brought her to the club became enraged. He assaulted two club employees and threatened to come back and kill the Director.

    The Frenchman, a black belt karate expert, was arrested less than 48 hours later for brandishing a .44 Magnum revolver. He was released on bail and I was assigned to protect the Director.

    Two nights later the Frenchman returned at the club's entrance with another man. I informed him in a businesslike manner that he was disallowed access to the club and that the Director would not see him. He and the other fellow left without incident.

    Two days passed and he returned, saying that he wanted the director (in less polite terms). He continued this while circling the club in his Porsche. Next, the Frenchman parked directly across from the entrance and remained in the car, silent for 7 minutes.

    At the onset, the Director had been moved to a safe room, the back door was secured with a person constantly monitoring it, and the police were called.

    The steel-framed entrance door with one window on the left was held at a .45-degree angle with my left foot in the hope of deflecting an incoming bullet. My right hand was on my weapon in the F.B.I. hip position and for the next 7 minutes the Frenchman and I looked each other in the eye.

A police cruiser passed between us after about 6 minutes, but elected not to stop. About a minute later, the Frenchman departed the area and he did not return.

I suspect that this had more to do with honor than with fear of death. You see, to the Frenchman, This was a matter of honor to be settled with the Director, and not with a security agent whom he had nothing personally against.

I am quite sure there was mutual respect between us during those 7 minutes where we were in opposition to each other's purpose. I am thankful that he elected to disengage, who knows what might have happened had he not.

4. The Bodyguard at the hospital:

A woman was shot and hospitalized in 1982 at a large hospital in northern Virginia. Her husband who attempted to murder her, threatened to come back and finish the job.

When I received the call from the hospitals Director of Security and Safety, I was asked to get there, "armed and fast."

When I arrived, I was briefed on the situation and led to the woman in intensive care who had been shot. The Director stipulated that I would be the only person armed in the hospital. Two deputy sheriffs who had been there prior to my arrival left the building.

There was only one way for the criminal to get to the woman. He had to pass down a corridor and turn a corner about 40 feet away from the door where I was standing.

My plan, if the criminal came around that corner armed, I would attempt to stop him with one well-placed head shot.

I was ill equipped for the job, armed with an accurized .45 automatic and three magazines of Match FMJ plus one of the same in the chamber. Such a bullet can pass through an individual and into something or someone else with damaging effect.

Among other things that entered into the picture was the fact that oxygen, gunpowder, and full metal-jacketed bullets do not mix unless you want results of disastrous proportions.

Six hours had passed when I got the word that the felon had been arrested on the way to the hospital.

5. An attempted abduction:

The place is a historic college town in northern Virginia and the main downtown street for merchants in that city. A young woman of college age was walking down the street when an intoxicated man emerged from a bar and grabbed her. As he forced her toward his car, she resisted, shouting "rape" repeatedly, and yelling "somebody help me". At this point, the abductor punched her in the stomach repeatedly, grabbed her by the collar of her blouse and the back of her belt and slammed her head into the concrete curb.

As I stepped out the doorway of a nearby shop, I saw the semi-conscious woman shaking her head in an attempt to regain full consciousness. The abductor was preparing to slam her head into the curb a second time when I drew my lawfully concealed revolver and said, "that's enough" in a commanding voice.

This diverted the abductors attention away from the girl and toward me. The owner of the bar took the woman to safety as her attacker approached me saying, "go ahead and shoot, that thing won't hurt me". The assailant came within about five yards of me before veering off to his car.

During this engagement, there were several bystanders in the street who were there before I was, and who were much closer to the criminal activity. Not one of them would help, but when the police arrived, one of them pointed me out saying, "He had a gun". Had the police officers not known me, the implications of that comment could have been severe.

Fortunately, there were other witnesses to confirm that my actions were in defense of life. The last question the officers asked was, "why didn't you shoot the guy's tires out?" I replied, "I had concerns about one of the bullets ricocheting into one of the bystanders 20 degrees to the right."

6. A massive firepower shoot-out in New York:

One innocent person was murdered in the presence of police officers, a police woman took a hit in her bullet-proof vest at about the same time as a lengthy mobile gun battle ensued that endangered the lives of dozens of police officers and God knows how many citizens. I doubt that anyone knows how many rounds were fired in this battle, but at least 150 shots were documented (130+ by the police alone).

The murderer was shot 18 times in non-vital areas of his body with a .38 Special semi-wadcutter bullets and was still running when he was shot to death by an officer armed with a shotgun loaded with slugs at a distance of approximately 20 feet. The officer armed with the shotgun missed with his first shot and concluded the action with his second, a headshot.

7. Escape from S.W.A.T.:

The barricaded criminal starts shooting through the wall with a .45 automatic pistol and wipes out a S.W.A.T. team in the process of making his escape, which was quite successful. Officers arrested him without incident about two months after the shooting.

8. Shoot-out in Miami:

   Two F.B.I. agents' dead, several more wounded, and finally two criminals killed in a lengthy gun battle.

   The two criminals were armed with a .223 semi-automatic rifle and a shotgun. The one with the rifle did most of the shooting, with a lot of ammunition being fired in a residential neighborhood.

   The two agents who died were killed while reloading according to reports.

   The criminal with the rifle was hit fatally with one or more of 13 shots to his body, yet he kept on shooting until shot again by another agent armed with a revolver during an attempt to escape in an F.B.I. car.

9. The attempt on President Reagan:

   When John Hinckley fired those shots that wounded the President, Secretary Brady, a Secret Service agent, and a Police officer there was no return fire. The action was over in about 2 seconds.

   Hinckley, who managed to covertly infiltrate the press area, was close, too close.

   The bullet that wounded the President deflected off the car. Secretary Brady and others took direct hits.

   Nobody saw it coming; the agents were forced to react while the bullets were flying.

   In the final analysis, Hinckley got his gun into action fast, fired his shots rapidly, and made them count even if only by luck (very bad luck for those directly involved).

10. An attempt on President Ford:

    President Ford stepped from the hotels entrance in San Francisco and a shot was fired from across the street. The .38 caliber bullet went high.

    Sarah Moore, the would-be assassin, was carried through the doors of the hotel sideways and taken to a conference room for interrogation. She declined to answer any questions until her son was picked up from school.

    When she did speak, two statements were memorable:

"I knew I shot high; if I had my .45. I would have hit him. It is a shame that if a person wants to make a political statement in this country, they have to do something like this."

President Ford escaped death by just a few feet that day.

11. The Sadat Assassination:
As the military parade passed, the President of Egypt looked on…

Men from the back of a military personnel carrier exited and fired automatic weapons into the Grandstand. Many of the people present thought it was part of some sort of exhibition, until they saw the blood.

The bulletproof partition was not in place, and the Egyptian President was dead as a result of overwhelming firepower and stealth.

12. The farm family of six that died:

As they entered the house, they were not aware of the burglary in progress by three escaped convicts.

The five men were executed one by one. The woman was taken to the woods a few miles away, raped, and then executed.

The three scumbags who committed this atrocity were sentenced to death. Too bad the victims were unable to defend themselves with firearms. A gun is only useful if you have it available when you need it.

13. Murder at a traffic light:

Two motorists angered with each other's actions stop at a traffic light. The driver of car #1 approaches the driver of car #2 and asks if he has a problem.

The driver of car #2 replies, "Yeah, you" and shoots the driver of car #1 to death. The driver from car #1 should have never left his car, though it would have benefitted him to distance himself from his killer with the accelerator pedal.

14. The double taps of death:

One armed man against three shoots the first one twice, and the second one once before being shot to death by the third.

The lone defender had time to fire three shots. Unfortunately for him, he fired one of them at the wrong target.

15. The duel that killed two:

There was an armed robbery in progress and the defender fired first. The large caliber handgun bullet noted for it's stopping power struck the robber in the head. The robber was dead in short order. So was the defender.

Either through electrical impulse, reflexive action, or deliberate fire, just prior to the instant of death, the robber fired one shot that struck the defender in the neck.

16. The drug bust that killed one out of two:

    This shooting was contributed by associate Greg Parrish who was directly involved in the action.

    Two armed individuals were encountered as they entered the garage via the side door. Greg took the one on the right out with his Browning High-Power loaded with Federal JHP's; one in the leg, the other in the shoulder. The subject was effectively stopped and lived to stand trial.

    His friend wasn't as fortunate. Greg's partner shot the 6'7", .45 Colt Commander armed opponent with one round of Speer CCI Lawman 200gr. JHP ammunition from his Star PD. The bullet impacted over the heart of the recipient who backed up against a garage door, and slid down it without further movement. The autopsy revealed that the individual had been on PCP when shot, and the slug that killed him expanded to better than 70 caliber.

17. Shoot-out at the Lake Tahoe Casino:

    The armed robber was shooting up the casino with his sub-machinegun. Fortunately, it jammed. A security officer (the only armed one in the place) shot him in the main body with his revolver.

    The robber, who was wearing body armor, pulled a backup handgun and fled the casino. Two police officers that had just arrived in the parking lot engaged the criminal in a gunfight.

    One officer took cover as the other officer fired at the criminal. The criminal was finally stopped after being wounded in the leg by one of the officer's .45 ACP Silvertip slugs.

    The action was over in the time it took the other officer to reach cover, according to reports.

18. The San Ysidro McDonalds massacre:

    A security officer (not employed by McDonalds) enters the restaurant with an Uzi carbine and opens fire.

A S.W.A.T. team surrounds the establishment as the victims lay bleeding to death on the floor.

The S.W.A.T. commander is on route to the scene, but will not give the police snipers a "Green Light" to neutralize the murderer until his arrival on the scene quite sometime later.

The victims were incapable of defending themselves and the police were of damn little assistance in this regard.

19. The Palm Bay Massacre:

An intoxicated gunman at a grocery store opens fire with a Ruger Mini-14 rifle.

A postal worker about 50 yards away shoots at the gunman with his .45 automatic pistol. He misses with all shots. This leads police to believe the two gunmen were acting together.

The gunman, upon arrival, shot the first police officer on the scene to death. The bullet went through the windshield, through the officer's hand, through the microphone in his hand, and into his head.

The second officer on the scene exited his car, shot his revolver empty from a distance of about 70 yards and was subsequently shot through the door of his police cruiser in his knee. The wounded officer crawled behind his patrol car as the criminal gunman ran 70 yards towards him. The gunman rolled the officer's body over with his foot, and fired five more shots into the officer's chest, killing him.

Sixteen people were shot by the criminal gunman, leaving six dead. A police sniper could have shot the gunman at several different times during the engagement, but the commander would not give him a "Green Light" to neutralize the criminal. Mr. Cruz, the murderer, was incarcerated at taxpayer expense. The victims have received substantially less government support.

20. An arrest and a shooting:

Two F.B.I. agents made the arrest of a suspect when another armed individual ran toward the scene. At the distance involved, the approaching individual resembled the description of a second suspect. The individual kept coming despite reported warnings from an F.B.I. agent, who then fired and fatally shot that person. As two agents approached, the one who fired the fatal shot came to the realization that he had just shot a third F.B.I. agent who was present at the scene. Robin was her name.

DEADLY ASSAULT

"Never look like what you are,
Anything is a threat,
And everything is a target."

> A former Marine in Florida
> Who is quite deadly with a
> Silenced MAC-10
>
> He carried it in a grocery bag.

There are several different types of deadly assault and with a few exceptions; they all have one thing in common—extreme violence.

Remote Assault:
Usually characterized by a bombing arranged by an individual who is not in the immediate area when it goes off, or by a sniper firing from some distance away. The J.F.K. assassination is an example of remote assault, so are car bombings. Sad to say, but advanced security and luck are the best defense against these actions.

Blitz Assault:
Characterized by multiple assailants assaulting from multiple directions. A constant visual awareness of your surroundings, advance detection, and superior defensive capability are the only hope of defense against this type of assault. The second stage of the assault led by the Israelis at Entebbe is an example of this type of assault.

Covert Assault:
Consists of an individual or individuals implanted in a manner that does not appear to be a threat. The action is usually swift and unforeseen at the onset. Difficult and perhaps impossible to detect beforehand, instantaneous neutralization and a lot of luck are the only hope of defense against such actions. The attempt on President Reagan by John Hinckley is an example of covert assault.

Dynamic Assault:
Characterized by extreme violence and continuous forward movement against the target. This type of assault may involve one or more individuals. Advance or instant detection and neutralization are imperative for survival against this type of action.

The embassy rescue conducted by British S.A.S. personnel is an example of dynamic assault. The S.A.S. commandos kept going violently through the embassy until they regained control of it. On that day, to their credit, they were unstoppable.

Escalated Assault:
Characterized by deteriorated social circumstances that become progressively more violent in scope. In almost all cases, there is a warning if you know how to read the signs. Best defense—when in doubt, find a way out. If something doesn't look right, it probably isn't.

The worst of all worlds is when you have a situation where characteristics of different types of assaults are combined. In the Sadat assassinations, Blitz, Dynamic, and Covert assault were combined. Much to our horror and dismay, we saw the results on national television.

METHODS FOR SURVIVAL

"You do what you have to, it's kill or be killed."

-Anonymous

The following thoughts and practices may be of assistance someday in surviving a lethal encounter.

SURVIVING ARMED ACTIONS

1) Have the fastest close-up shot capability—a Smith & Wesson Model 638 in your jacket pocket or purse with your hand on it at the onset of an engagement. Shoot through the purse or jacket pocket if necessary. A piece of cardboard covered with cloth will break up the guns outline if placed between the gun and the outside of the jacket pocket for maximum concealment. This is the fastest close range delivery system in existence with a first shot capability of one-fifth of a second or less for many individuals.

2) Learn to shoot straight and fast from a good instructor and practice regularly. Learn to deliver accurate fire from any position you may find yourself in at the onset of a deadly encounter.

3) Select the most powerful weapon that you can control effectively as a second gun and use ammunition with a good record of stopping aggression in gunfights.

4) Stay alert, detect your problem before it is a problem and make preparations in advance.

5) Use defensive movement to your advantage whenever possible and prudent to do so. Dive for cover, deflect the attackers weapon, run or crouch when left in the open if this is justified under the conditions involved. Do anything that will enhance your chances of surviving the encounter.

6) Employ stealth if at all possible. Stay silent, invisible, odorless and out of the way. Let the attacker expose himself to you, not vice-versa.

7) Be prepared to act defensively should the need arise. Do not freeze up. Your survival instincts may come into play here, affecting your mental process. If they do, do not fight it, go with the mental brain-flow, and do whatever it takes to survive.

8) Have a weapon and ammunition that goes "bang" every time. If the gun or ammunition you are using in practice sessions malfunctions, do not trust it with your life. Correct the problem or get a new system.

9) Have a quality weapon design with a proven record in actual combat that has stood the test of time.

10) Have an accurate weapon on hand, one that shoots where you want it to.

11) Have good tactical stopping and penetrating capability from your weapon/ammunition combination. Maximize your capability and use it intelligently. The loads recommended earlier in this section are excellent in this respect for their particular caliber.

12) Your weapon should be highly controllable in your hands. Forget about .44 Magnums, and rocket launchers. You may need a fast 2nd, 3rd, 4th, or 5th shot.

13) Have weapons (plural) with sufficient firepower for any defensive engagement you may find yourself in. An empty gun is the last thing you want in your hand in a gunfight. They tend to be found in the hands of dead men.

14) Your gun should be quiet in operation prior to firing and should not be visible in the dark. Avoid light colored guns for defensive purposes.

15) You and your gun should be as one. The weapon must point well for you. You may not be able to see the sights in the darkness.

16) Have your own gun available when you need it. That means constantly.

17) Make good use of tactics whenever possible and develop the knowledge to do this intelligently. If you can shoot an armed assailant through the wall without endangering innocent persons, do so. Whatever the tactical opportunity at hand, if it gives you an edge in the fight, use it.

18) If cover is close at hand, get behind it and stay back a few feet from it if possible. A notable exception would be a street curb. In that case, stay in close. Ironically, the time to throw yourself in the gutter may come at the onset of a gunfight, and that move has saved lives.

19) Stay away from walls. Bullets bounce off them and into human flesh.

20) Keep yourself in the dark and the attacker illuminated when it is possible to do this without exposing your position.

21) Select your position carefully, if you have the chance. Use terrain intelligently when possible. Channel the approach by the attacker if you can do so in a manner that presents the least possible risk for yourself.

22) When dealing with multiple armed attackers, take them out in tactical order. If you are behind cover, take them out as they appear without exposing yourself to more than one at a time. If you are in the open, take out the most immediate threat first. If the attackers pose an equal threat, take them out fast with one shot each, with additional shots delivered to any who still remain a threat.

23) Make use of a diversion if you perceive it to be to your advantage in a defensive encounter.

24) Don't stick around after your muzzle flash has exposed your position in darkness. MOVE, FAST.

Have a strong will to live, and keep shooting until the threat has ended.

Keep one other thing in mind, as former Secretary of Defense McNamara once proclaimed, sometimes "the best defense, is a strong offense."

On February 25, 1836, Samuel Colt patented his revolver. It has been said that God created men, and Sam Colt made them equal. May the forces of God and Colt be with you when you need them most.

SECTION 3

THE STEALTH SYSTEM

OF PERSONAL DEFENSE WITH FIREARMS

Every year, police officers and decent citizens are victimized by armed criminals in America.

For the police officer, this is often due to administrative restrictions, and status quo regulated training.

The private citizen is often subjected to media hype and misinformation in a deliberate attempt to limit his knowledge and capabilities.

Criminals pay little or no attention to regulations and restrictions. They are not affected by the regulations and restrictions placed upon our nations law enforcement officers.

Private citizens do not need limited knowledge and capabilities when facing an armed and dangerous criminal with murderous intent. They need maximum defensive capability.

I liken this situation to black holes in outer space. Such holes, astronomers tell us, can suck things down them faster than the speed of light and completely destroy them in the process.

My uncle, by contrast, spent many hours flying and testing jet aircraft for the U.S. military. He once related the following story to me: "Every once in awhile, I'd see a hole in the clouds with the sun shining through it, and when I did, I'd take my airplane through it as fast as I could. It was the greatest feeling of freedom I've ever had, and something few people ever experience."

In the following pages, we'll take it to the limit, and hopefully provide you with greater freedom from fear of dangerous criminals. This book can help turn things around, so that black hole is facing the criminal, instead of you.

A SUPERIOR SYSTEM OF SAFETY

1) Always handle your weapon in the manner you would a loaded gun. If you think it's unloaded, check it and recheck it.

2) Never point a gun at anything you do not want to see destroyed, or it may be.

3) Keep your finger off the trigger until you are ready to discharge the weapon.

4) Be certain of your target, what is behind it, and the penetration capabilities of the cartridge you are using.

5) Know your weapon, its safe carry modes, safety features, operating characteristics and limitations.

6) Wear ear and eye protection on the range.

WHEN HANDLING THE WEAPON FOR CLEANING OR INSPECTION, ALWAYS CHECK TO SEE IF IT IS LOADED THREE TIMES.

CHECK IT THREE TIMES…

THREE TIMES.

THREAT RECOGNITION

How do you know of approaching danger?

You know when something does not look, feel, smell, sound, or taste right. In a word: abnormalities.

A heightened sense of awareness can warn you of a dangerous presence. So can knowledge of what is possible.

When a human (non-motorized) threat is ten feet or more in distance from you, watch the hands of that perceived dangerous individual. At the distance involved, any attack by the threat must be delivered via the hands.

At closer distances, your recognition capabilities are reduced, though certain defensive options are enhanced. The close-in threat has greater attack flexibility, which must be defeated by lightning fast reflexive action, superior defensive movement and capability. The good news is that you have equally flexible defense options if you know them in advance of the attack. None-the-less, distance, more often than not is your friend.

For any move that an attacker can make, there is a defensive move that can counter it if the knowledge and capability are present at the moment.

Playing defense is always harder, but offensive advantage is reduced if the approach can be determined, and superior counter-action channeled by you.

A short time ago, I provided special defensive instruction to a correctional officer in Nevada. After lunch, this impressive young man asked, "Tony, what is the most important of the five senses?"

My response—"the sixth one!"

THE HIDDEN THREAT

Criminals are becoming more sophisticated these days. I know of at least three examples where "sleepers" (criminals who blend in with bystanders or appear to be a bystander) killed police officers that had countered the initial apparent criminal activity. In each instance, the murdered officers failed to recognize potential danger beyond the suspects at hand.

Peripheral awareness from a protected position could have saved them.

Develop the awareness to see and sense the invisible threat, and remember the ominous words of a former Marine in Florida with a silenced MAC-10 sub-machinegun:

> "Never look like what you are, anything is a threat, and everything is a target."

He carries the MAC in a grocery bag with several loaded magazines, and is quite deadly with it.

His statement is the essence of The Stealth System.

Remember it!

OPTIMUM PROTECTIVE CAPABILITY

This condition exists only when maximum personal ability and maximum emergency equipment capability are interrelated.

Consider the following example:

The man is extensively trained and practiced in all methods and elements outlined in this book.

In his right jacket pocket is a Smith and Wesson 638 fitted with custom grips and a factory hammer shroud. He can deliver five shots with this concealed weapon in less than 1.5 seconds to kill zone of a man-size target by firing through the pocket at close range. He can deliver the first shot in one-fifth of a second or less. Complete concealment is afforded by cardboard placed between the gun and the outside of his jacket pocket.

In his left jacket pocket is a Smith and Wesson Model 638 Bodyguard concealed in the same manner and with the same capabilities. Now we have two concealed revolvers in the hands of an experienced man who can deliver two shots in one-fifth of a second or less, ten shots in 1.5 seconds or less; fired simultaneously in different directions if desired. That's getting close to a sub-machinegun's rate of fire, with greater flexibility. Not bad for an introduction.

With ten shots gone in 1.5 seconds, back-up firepower might be needed in the event of continued action or a more distant encounter. Our man reaches for his custom Browning 9mm concealed behind his right hip, and he can now deliver an additional 21 rounds of 9mm anti-terrorist ammunition to a man-size target seven yards downrange in less than four seconds. Several spare 20 round magazines are available to him via tension release holders. Long range and enhanced penetrations rounds are contained in some of these magazines. The weapon when loaded with these rounds is capable of four-inch groups at 100 yards in this man's hands.

His vehicle, which is bullet resistant from the rear, houses a S.O.A.R.S. (Special Operations Automatic Rifle System). On those occasions where the situation warrants it, this highly developed weapon can be concealed under his trench coat with a special sling, ready for immediate use. This weapon features: Telescopic night sight, minute of angle accuracy, reduced muzzle flash and recoil, 20 and 30 round magazine capability, and optional operational encasement capability. The size of this weapon is actually smaller than many sub-machine guns, it is just as controllable, and it has range capabilities out to 500 yards with excellent penetration characteristics.

On those occasions where a lower operational profile is desired, the Model 638 S & W can be carried in the side pants pocket with a back-up capability in the other side pants pocket. With his hand on the gun at the onset of a confrontation, lightning fast draws and first shots at close range can be delivered without notice of intent.

If he has to walk into a dangerous situation that might require instantaneous response with greater mobility and accuracy potential, he can place the S & W 638 into a quality paper bag that is folded properly, and with invisible incisions cut in the area of the trigger guard. Additional incisions on the bag along the top of the gun enable sight usage with a tug on the bottom of the bag. The gun can be carried ready to fire through the bag instantly in total invisibility.

The advantages of such a system are considerable and it can be tailored to the individuals needs.

A merchant, for example, might find the paper bag technique most useful, as might the courier or detective on special assignment. A police officer might feel more comfortable approaching potentially dangerous suspects with his hand in his pocket holding a revolver on those suspects. All of the options would comfort the bodyguard.

The Stealth System affords unmatched first shot delivery speed and superior overall capability in an invisible package. This is the Stealth Advantage.

DIVERSIONS

Envision the following:

You are in complete darkness, and silent with gun in hand after hearing shots fired in the business complex where you work. The initial shots fired by a disgruntled co-worker killed two of your fellow workers and short-circuited the electricity.

Now the killer is coming after you. You can occasionally detect his movement through noise but not enough to give you an exact location. The only escape is past the area where the initial shots were fired, and noise from the killer's movements has been coming from that direction. What would you do?

Here is what I would do:

1) I would take an object that could be tossed silently and that would make noise when it hit.
2) I would throw that object a safe distance in a direction away from the killer and me.
3) I would watch for his muzzle flash and fire several shots in that area rapid fire.
4) I would move rapidly and quietly (shoes removed) around the most distant perimeter of the room in a U-type fashion, escape, and notify the authorities.

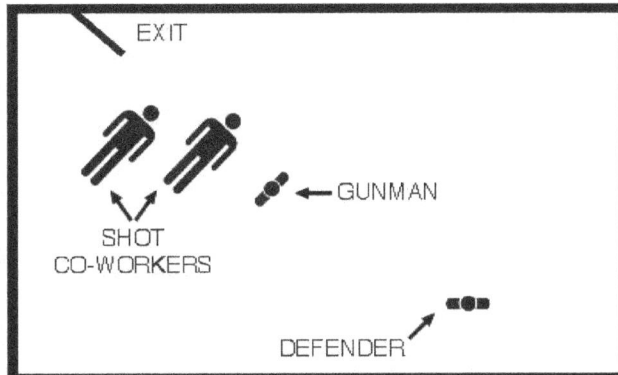 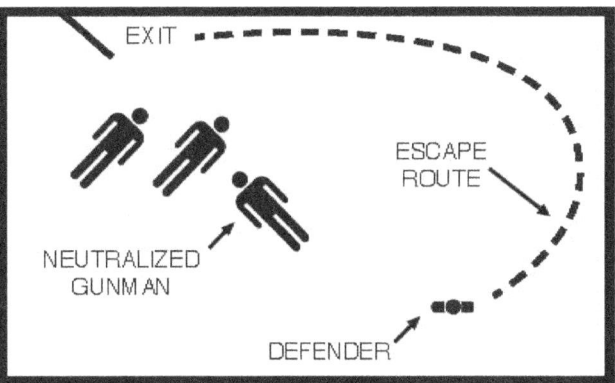

The objective is to keep as much distance as possible between you and the attacker without giving away your position.

If you are ever in the unfortunate position of being held at gunpoint from a distance greater than point blank, without a gun in your hand, a glance over the criminal's shoulder with a smile on your face may give you a fighting chance.

STEALTH CAPABILITIES IN PROTRACTED ENGAGEMENTS

Harmless.

Odorless.

Silent.

Invisible.

Out of the way.

This is the target that stealth presents.

The elements work

Undetectable targets don't get shot as a rule.

One other thing to consider:

The target that stealth presents, properly equipped, is the most dangerous and deadly target of all…

BULLET DEFLECTION

Knowledge of how bullets work when they strike can provide you with substantial advantages under the right conditions.

A bullet of conventional design will travel straight in line with the flat surface it impacts upon if delivered to that surface at a shallow angle.

In short, you may be able to ricochet your bullets into an attacker while affording yourself greater safety in the process of doing so.

If the threat is using a car for cover, deflected fire off the pavement may be the only way of reaching the target.

If the threat is at a 90° angle on the opposite side of a wall and several feet downrange against the wall, why not bounce a couple shots off the wall and into the threat while minimizing your exposure to danger.

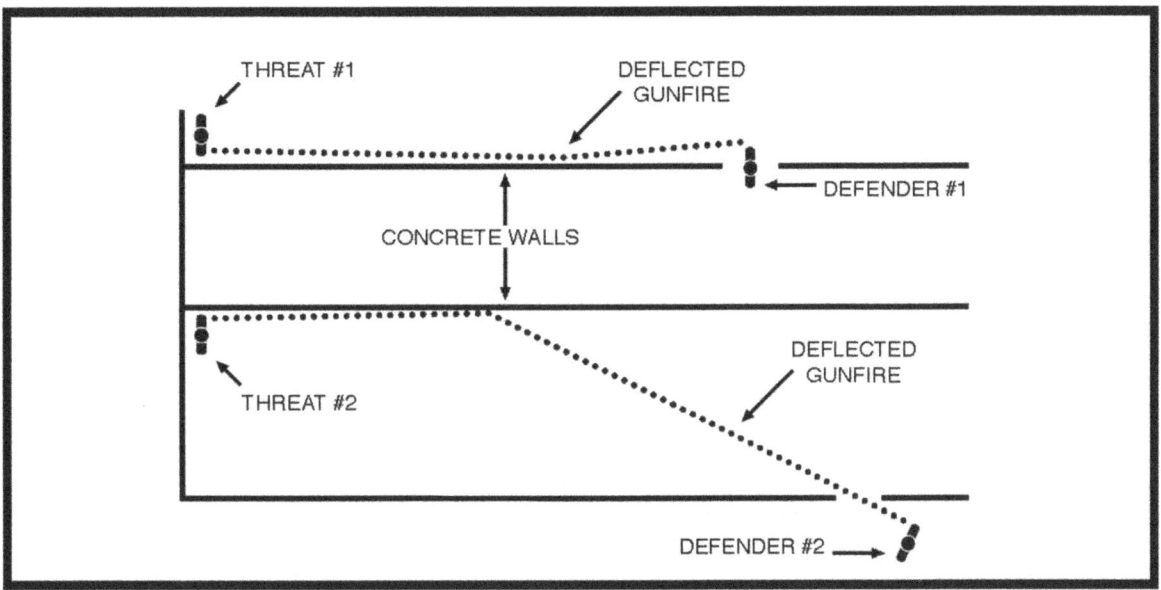

Walls are great under the right conditions if you know how to use them to your advantage in a gunfight, but don't be caught dead standing next to one.

PENETRATION ANALYSIS

In terms of getting through hard cover to the bad guy, keep in mind, it is not just what can get through, but what you have left after you get through. Full metal jacket ammo as used by the military gives you maximum penetration capability against hard targets; some rounds with steel jackets enhance penetration even more.

The 158gr. +P Winchester S.W.H.P. is my all-around choice in .38 Special snubs that will handle it. Glaser safety slugs in this caliber make sense where minimal penetration characteristics are desired. I make it a practice to carry one round of Glaser in my S & W 638 under the hammer. By exerting minimal trigger pressure, I can rotate the cylinder one notch so that the Glaser will be the first round fired should special penetration characteristics be desired.

In .223, the M-855 is the ultimate performer with Remington 55gr. J.H.P. in reserve for situations where minimal penetration is desired.

These cartridges offer enhanced capability within the system, and that is important because when things get serious—it's either a no go or balls to the wall.

CLOSE RANGE COUNTER-MEASURES AND THREAT NEUTRALIZATION

At the onset of a fight where you are close enough to touch your adversary and are only dealing with one, punch him in the nose with the palm of a karate fist while taking a step back with the foot below your primary gun hand, then retract a clenched fist to your chest, then keep the weapon close to your side and discharge it if warranted. Use this technique prior to the attackers completed draw.

If you are being held at gunpoint and are able to, deflect the attackers weapon with your non-shooting hand by grasping the attackers wrist, and pushing it away from your body while simultaneously pivoting your body out of the line of fire and using your weapon on the assailant. This must be done lightening fast to avoid being shot.

High-level specialists have rendered the opinion that the only way to instantly neutralize a deadly human threat is to disrupt the upper spine and/or brain. Even that may not work in every instance (though it has in the vast majority).

The medulla oblongata is the part of the brain that controls motor functions. This pear-shaped organ, also known as the brain stem, is located at the base of the skull. Frontal shots delivered to this organ will pass through the neck or mouth areas of the recipient. Side shots should be aimed just below and to the rear of the earlobe. A hostage situation can be best resolved from the rear by delivering a centered shot to the base of the skill of the criminal involved. Where immediate close range threat neutralization is essential, the medulla oblongata is the target of choice if reasonable hit probability exists under the circumstances. This target requires a precise controlled shot.

What if you are facing multiple armed attackers at close range? That is where those two shrouded hammer revolvers in your side pockets are in a class by themselves. Take them out, two at a time.

COVER AND CONCEALMENT

Concealment is defined as material that hides you from a dangerous aggressor and gives you a measure of stealth that can be used to defeat the threat or perhaps evade it.

Cover is defined as material that will stop an opponents bullets before they get to you. Body armor can be thought of in terms of partial constant cover. Make use of it, and insist on level two and above only.

The concept of leverage is important when using cover. You don't want to be right up against it in most cases, but there are exceptions such as street curbs. On the other hand, you don't want to be far away from it because then it becomes a form of cover to your adversary. Under most conditions, three to seven feet is about what I would use depending on the distance of my opponent, and the nature of the cover.

Incidentally, if you know an armed aggressors position behind concealment, such as a wall, and the fire zone will not endanger innocents on the other side, why not shoot through the wall? A friend of mine who is a police officer did, and his problem no longer existed.

Use of cover is generally enhanced while standing using the Weaver Stance due to its bladed position. Right and left hand corners require a different technique where the gun hand is farther from the corner. A quarter circle movement from low ready, and a 45° hold going past the corner can enhance your hit potential on your non-dominant hand side.

Other instances where you might want to be closer to cover include trees, telephone poles, and mail boxes.

Using a vehicle, get behind the engine block. Use positions like prone, kneeling, sitting, and squatting where appropriate due to cover height.

COVERING, CONTAMINATION, AND SUPPRESIVE FIRE

Suppressive fire is defined as shots fired in rapid succession to discourage return fire on the part of opponents, thereby enabling the shooter(s) to advance on an enemy position.

Suppressive fire is most useful in neutralizing a protected fire point in conjunction with flanking.

Contamination fire is gunfire directed at and intended to saturate a given area.

Contamination fire is most useful for stopping an advancing attacker at close range and saturation of areas containing hostile targets.

Covering fire consists of shots fired in rapid succession to discourage shooting by opponents while the shooter and/or others move to a different location.

Covering fire is useful in providing safer mobility out of certain danger.

All have their place and purpose, and all are interrelated in that they all require massive firepower capability.

FIREPOWER

A high level of firepower offers the shooter flexibility in an armed action. It also offers him peace of mind.

The most disconcerting and frightening feeling in an armed fight is holding an empty gun while the action is still going on.

A second and third gun can help insure that you won't find yourself in that position. Even then, rapid reloading capability should be an integral part of your system.

In April of 1986, several F.B.I. agents in Miami engaged two highly trained (military and police trained) criminal gunmen in a gunfight. Before the criminals expired from their wounds, they fired more than fifty rounds, killing two and wounding another five F.B.I. agents in the process.

The shotgun-armed criminal fired only one round in this fight, with the balance fired by the rifleman, Platt.

F.B.I. agents fired better than fifty shots in this action prior to neutralizing the criminals.

Special Agent Dove had already fired somewhere in the neighborhood of thirty rounds when he was killed while reloading an empty gun.

The action lasted about four minutes.

Remember that the next time someone tells you, "Six shots are enough".

Let the others have their six, you make damn sure you've got sixty plus.

THE CONTROLLED SHOT

If I were being held hostage at gunpoint and I had my choice of rescuers, I would pick the French Anti-Terrorist personnel over all others.

Why?

Their very special capacity for making the controlled shot under extraordinary circumstances.

These men are trained to place a critical shot exactly where they want it to go and very little, if anything is left to error.

How good are they?

At the end of training sessions, these men have worn clay pigeon-type necklaces over their body armor and shot each other over the heart with full power. 357 Magnum ammunition, at an impressive distance.

In matters of life and death, these Frenchmen don't miss.

It is a matter of honor to them.

Shouldn't it be to you?

When dealing with a hostage rescue situation. If you cannot make the shot, do not take the shot.

THE PROTECTED POSITION

Imagine standing behind a bulletproof partition that is transparent with a firing port built into it, and having an armed attacker assault that position from the other side, unaware.

The results are predictable.

In real life, the average person won't be that fortunate. He may, however, be able to place himself in a position that offers relative safety from deadly threats.

Angled doors and metal that can deflect bullets offer increased safety.

Locations and angles that put you in a position to strike but leave the attacker defenseless stack the deck against criminals. A certain amount of leverage is involved here, and the illustration below will help in understanding this principle.

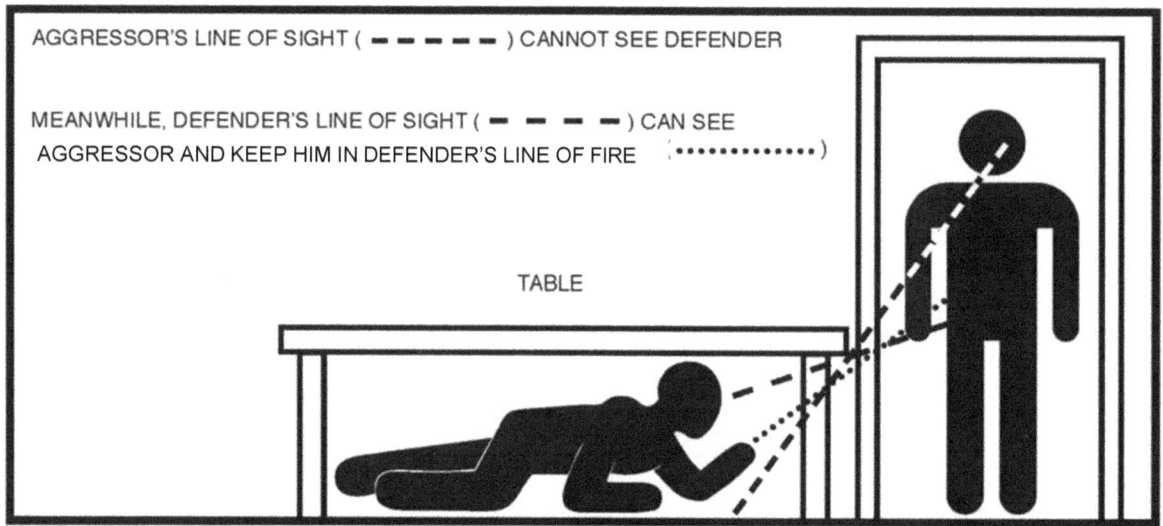

Full directional fire capability should be maintained at all times (being able to fire in any direction). You never know where a hostile target might show up.

Another consideration is weapon retention for the uniformed officer. If pressure is applied against the weapon with the forearm while tucking the thumb of the gun hand in the belt, weapon retention is enhanced and the draw is not impaired.

FIRE ZONES AND THE PERIMETER OF THE CRISIS POINT

A fire zone is nothing more than the area exposed to gunfire. The laws of physics will limit it and limitations may also be imposed by the shooter(s) and/or terrain.

The crisis point in this instance can be best defined as the area of immediate danger.

If you can extricate yourself from the crisis point or the criminals fire zones, you are safe.

In many cases, it is prudent to do this, and I might add, that it almost always makes sense to avoid entering such areas to begin with. Sometimes crisis points are like those black holes in outer space. Once in, you don't come out…

Of course, the ideal situation exists when your fire zones can reach the criminal, but his can't reach you. This can sometimes be accomplished by deflected gunfire, and sometimes by other means such as barriers that expose the threat to you but not vice versa.

That is the greatest stealth advantage of all.

THE PREPARED STATE OF MIND

I don't know that anything can prepare anyone for an encounter where the individual is caught off guard.

The key is not to be.

If you are surprised, you may suffer momentary shock, followed by time distortion (slow-motion) and other possible distortions of your perception.

I have been in several life threatening situations, and I experienced the above symptoms in only one of them; the first one. In that situation, I was not expecting the series of events that occurred. Stealth on the part of my adversary was involved. Even so, keen awareness, and cool, calm, deliberate response overcame the initial shock.

When a person has been exposed to deadly danger and has prepared for any eventuality, that person has nothing to fear. Concentration is centered on countering the threat at hand, and implementing the best possible way to do so.

THE LEGALITIES

You must fear for your life or the life of another and have a valid reason to do so before you can use deadly force in defense of life.

General Thoughts for Dealing with the Police in the Aftermath of a Shooting or Violent/Armed Confrontation immediately after the Incident

1. Check your surroundings for additional threats.
2. Watch the hands of any potential hostile adversaries in the area.
3. Seek cover if possible if you are not already behind it.
4. Move exposed weapons away from adversaries with your foot! (Step & slide without the muzzle of the weapon(s) crossing your other foot or other people).
5. Tell potential adversaries to keep their hands visible and not move.
6. Call the police.

The 911 Call

1. They may say police or fire. Ask for police
2. Give your name and location twice.
3. Give a brief description of events and your justified action. (i.e. An individual just broke into my home and threatened me with a gun. I had to shoot him twice in self-defense.).
4. Ask for an ambulance and police response.
5. Tell them you moved the attackers gun away from him with your foot so he would not shoot you with it.
6. Give them your description and the attacker(s) description.
7. Notify them that you are holding the attacker(s) at gunpoint if you are doing so and that you have not checked for additional weapons on the attacker.
8. Stay on the phone with the 911 dispatcher and maintain communication. Ask to be advised of police arrival, so that you can safely secure your gun when they get there.

When Police Arrive On Scene

1. Let them in with your gun secured in a non-threatening manner.
2. Point out evidence that is favorable to you (i.e. that is his gun over there, I moved it there with my foot so he would not shoot me with it. That is my gun on the table. He broke in through that window and I will sign the compliant against him. I am the homeowner.)
3. Politely invoke your Fifth Amendment rights (i.e. Officers this is a serious matter and you will have my full cooperation in 24 hours after I have spoken with legal counsel.)
4. If arrested in the aftermath, do not talk in your jail cell. They may put an undercover officer in there with you. They can legally lie to you but not vice versa.

5. You will be given one phone call that connects if arrested in the aftermath. It should go to the person who cares the most about you in this world. That person should know who you want representing you or how to find them. In this area I recommend Ms. Tammy Riggs. Her office is on California St. In areas where you do not know a good attorney, have your helper go down to the Courthouse and ask three (3) bailiffs whom the best Criminal Defense Attorney in town is. If you get the same name 2 or 3 times, that's the one.

Lastly, I recommend that you commit this information to memory rather than carry it on you. You do not want a prosecutor using it against you as a scripted response, or regular business record, which is admissible evidence in court.

SECTION 4

SELECTING YOUR DEFENSIVE SIDEARM

An Overview

Analysis of the suitability of handguns for defensive purposes is inherently a subjective undertaking. The facts and opinions contained within these pages are derived from actual usage of the guns tested by this author and others.

The test results were obtained on actual field service weapons and those sent to law enforcement agencies for testing. The results are not necessarily indicative of all firearms of like kind. It should be pointed out, however, that these results are based on millions of rounds fired through the various weapons tested.

Human beings vary in size, sensitivity, and ability with regard to weapon suitability for a particular individual. I have been able to observe the performance of various firearms in the hands of many different individuals, big and small, male and female, young and old. This does not mean that the results will be the same for you. As a high-level firearms instructor, I have seen variables among persons that preclude such certainty.

I will therefore, proceed to report on observations by myself and other qualified individuals and make those judgments necessary as best I can.

You should know; this project almost did not materialize. A business associate of mine in the Dallas, Texas area once told me, "Don't do anything to disturb the market; a man has got to have confidence in his weapon." His name is Dave and I respect him, but there is a flip side to his equation, which is the reason for this section. A man or a woman has to have a weapon he or she can have confidence in.

MAKING YOUR SELECTION

There are many things to consider when purchasing a weapon for personal protection.

Recoil (kick) sensitivity, whether or not the weapon will be carried on the person, and how the weapon performs for you are important considerations.

If you live in an area with a range that rents handguns, go there and shoot a .22, then move up to a 9mm, 40 S & W, .38, .45, and 357 Magnum. When the recoil starts affecting your performance, go down in size to the next lower caliber, and select the quality weapon that is right for you in that caliber.

All ammunition in the various calibers are not alike. Some cartridges in their respective caliber perform in a superior fashion. They sometimes cost more and they are worth it.

My recommendations are:

.22- CCI

.380- Federal Hydro Shok, Hornady XTP

.38 Special +P- Winchester 158gr. SWHP

9mm-124gr. +P Gold Dot

357 SIG- 125gr. JHP

.357 Magnum- Winchester 145gr. Silvertip

.45 ACP- Federal Match Hardball, Federal Hydro Shok or HST, Rem Golden Saber

40 S & W- Rem Golden Saber 165gr. or Speer Gold Dot 165gr.

*Ball rounds should be reserved in spare magazine for penetrating hard targets.

One last piece of lifesaving advice:

GET PROFFESSIONAL INSTRUCTION OF A HIGH ORDER—THE GUN IS ONLY AS EFFECTIVE AS YOU ARE.

I provide instruction through renoconcealedweapons.com

Firearm Selection

There has never been a better time for those U.S. firearms owners who live in the states and areas with minimal firearms restrictions. I strongly recommend that you join the NRA and Gun Owners of America if you wish to maintain those firearms rights.

There is a wider selection of top quality defensive weaponry available than at any other time in history.

There are also a number of less desirable products out there.

I will attempt to provide you with wisdom and guidance in the selection process.

The following are some general guidelines:

1) Avoid small handguns for primary weapons
2) Avoid heavy and long travel double action only handguns. Standard S & W M & P's Glocks and Springfield XD's **do not** fall into this category.
3) Avoid lower quality, low price manufacturers. You can buy a decent gun for $300.00 circa 2014. I would not go below that for defensive purposes.

Here are a number of primary handgun recommendations that I can give you that I have experience with.

1) Springfield XDm 4.5—I like the .40 S & W the best. Excellent power, controllability, firepower, and practical accuracy make this a top contender.
2) Smith and Wesson M & P 9mm and 40 S & W Full size and Compact. In my experience, they work well for most people if a little less controllable than the XDm 4.5.
3) Beretta 92fs/m-9—Excellent reliable, accurate, and controllable 9mm handgun. The standard U.S. Armed Forces Sidearm.
4) Sig 226—A top-notch 9mm handgun in every way. A variation, the MK-25, is the standard sidearm of the U.S. Navy Seals. The Sig 226 has also seen use with Blackwater and British S.A.S. anti-terrorist team personnel. I prefer the Elite SAO model.
5) Browning High Power 9mm—Superb single action 9mm handgun. It saw use by a number of top tier units; our C.I.A. Operatives who flew into Afghanistan to start the war were believed to have been armed with them.
6) High quality 1911 .45 pistols—Still a standard sidearm of several top tier professional units including FBI, SWAT, and HRT (hostage rescue team) units.
7) SIG P-229—Standard sidearm of the U.S. Secret Service in .357 Sig reportedly
8) CZ-75 9mm—A top performing 9mm.

Other good choices in my experience:

- Ruger P-95
- Taurus 809
- Glock 17 (Less desirable grip for me)
- Springfield XD Tactical 5"
- SIG Pro 2022 9mm
- FN FNX 9mm
- H & K USP
- FN Five-Seven (Also in use with U.S. Secret Service reportedly).

Any of the above listed guns would probably serve you well as a primary defensive handgun.

A good hammer shrouded revolver such as the Smith and Wesson Model 638 would make an excellent backup or secondary handgun.

Under certain circumstances a good Double-Action .357 revolver might be the top choice for certain tactical applications such as operational encasement. I believe the Ruger GP-100 in four to six inch barrels to be the best new all around choice for this type of requirement.

In general, I prefer a high capacity 9mm, 357 SIG, or 40 S & W auto pistol of top quality. With the armed gang members in society these days, you probably do not want less than 10 round capacity. 14 round capacity is better.

Purchase a quality capable and reliable handgun or two. Become proficient with it or them, and you should be well protected in a defensive emergency.

The Navy SEALS have a saying- two is one and one is none.

What the SEALS are saying is that if your primary handgun or weapon is disabled in a fight, and you have a second gun, you still have something to fight with. If not, you have nothing.

Secret Service used to have a saying as well—if it gets to the point where you have to use your gun, you probably have not done your job in the first place. Always avoid a fight and extricate yourself from fire zones or the crisis point if possible.

I sincerely hope you never find yourself in this type of situation. If you do, I hope you prevail.

I am told that Teddy Roosevelt once said, "The best thing you can do is the right thing, the second best thing you can do is the wrong thing, and the worst thing you can do is nothing." Good luck, and good shooting.

The Merlin Seven Project

Many years ago, I traveled to the HQ building for one of our government agencies tasked with diplomatic protection among other things in the Washington D.C. area. I met with their top weapons man and his assistant at that time, and showed them what was at the time a state-of-the-art weapons system with special application for diplomatic protection and airport security.

This weapon featured low light sighting capability, a computer designed muzzle brake which enabled rapid fire with little to no barrel movement, operational encasement capability (it could be fired through a custom built suitcase), and minute of angle custom tuned accuracy (it could put three consecutive shots into a U.S. quarter coin at 100 yards). That was Merlin One, known at the time as the S.O.A.R.S. (Special Operations Automatic Rifle System).

Their top weapons man informed me that the system was 30 percent better than what they were using, but that there were problems. He then said, "You can't mass produce it, and I have hundreds of what we are using now in inventory." That weapon was sold to an individual with a connection to the Fort Lewis Rangers who was very happy to have it.

One of my female clients expressed an interest in a handgun for personal protection with a reflex sight on it, after firing one of mine on the range.

I told her I would look into it.

To me, practicality in a protective handgun system would require constant sight illumination. That meant the Trijicon RMR would be the only sight meeting that long term criteria. The sight would have to be very rugged. The RMR is. The weapon would need to be very reliable.

Even though it would not be applicable to the average shooter, I wanted to demonstrate personal accuracy on a man size target at 80 yards.

My choice in caliber would be 9mm, as it is the one most commonly used with tier one professionals throughout the world. It is also a center fire caliber that most women find controllable, and do good work with.

I had originally planned to use a single action semi-automatic pistol due to the generally superb triggers found on such guns, and the inherent safety of the weapon when carried in condition two when one is equipped with a firing pin safety. I noticed in testing and development that the recoil arc was less desirable with this setup due to a higher bore in relation to the shooters hand. Subsequent testing with a Smith & Wesson M&P C.O.R.E. 9L with 5 inch barrel yielded much better results.

Early on in this project I requested one of the new Trijicon RMR (Ruggedized Miniature Reflex) sights with the 12.9 MOA triangular reticle. Trijicon came through in exceptional fashion. When

I received the sight, I was very impressed. Unlike other sights, this one is always operational and ready for use in light or dark conditions due to the dual illumination engineering of the sight.

In bright conditions, it operates off of fiber optic technology, while in darkness the reticle is self-illuminated with tritium gas. This is magical engineering that gives the good guys and gals an edge.

The Smith & Wesson M&P C.O.R.E. 9L is equipped with co-witness iron sights that are visible a little below the illuminated RMR triangle reticle. Testing revealed that Smith & Wesson got this right for two reasons:

1) The iron sights are always available as backup in the unlikely event of damage to the reflex sight.
2) Under certain conditions where an individual is in a dark environment and is aiming into a bright area, the reticle can wash out and become less visible or not visible at all. If that happens, the iron sights work perfectly.

There were other considerations in developing a weapons system like this.

First, the trigger system would need a foreign object protection in the carry mode, as the only safety is a passive one on the trigger.

Second, it seemed wise to have protective covering for the RMR sight, giving it additional protection from the elements.

Third, why not create an operational encasement enabling close range threat neutralization through the case if needed.

A modified day planner type unit fitted with a modified mount to eliminate gun movement within the case proved to be the solution to all three considerations so long as nothing else is placed in the gun compartment.

Everything was properly constructed, and testing and evaluation commenced. Past work for major defense contractors as part of testing and evaluation teams, and clearance of numerous buildings for the government would serve as excellent experience and guidance for this.

So at the end of the day, do we have a practical real world system for protective and defensive use?

The answer is a strong qualified yes with the following considerations:

1) Case retention adjustment and knowledge, and trigger finger indexing must be committed to memory.
2) Case carry methods and drawing technique must be fully ingrained in memory and practice.

3) Training and practice from ready positions to target or point ready must be practiced regularly almost exclusively with this weapon. This is especially important, because you have a narrow window of only a little angle to visualize the triangular reticle.

If you are not willing to commit to the foregoing, this system may fail you in a serious armed encounter.

If you are one of those people for whom a single plane sighting system works best, and you put the time in to do the practice, you will be rewarded with an exceptional system that will serve you well and provide you with advantages.

Many thanks to Trijicon; more than anyone else, they made this system possible. No other sight would do, and their superior quality, engineering, and development shows. Everyone I have shown this system to loves it!

Kudos also to Smith & Wesson, they got it right, and knowing what is involved, they did a great deal of research and development to get it right.

Thanks also to Master Custom Pistol Smith Terry Tussey who is truly one of the best in the world for his wise counsel and vast knowledge and experience.

Firearm Selection

Carbines, Rifles, and Shotguns

The FBI has issued high-powered rifles to their agents working in rural areas. At one time they issued pump action Remington 30-06 rifles.

The M-4 type carbine is in use by FBI personnel.

The A-2 M-16/AR-15 rifle was in use by the Air Force Base protection personnel in the 1990's.

The H&K 91 type rifle has a good record as a .308 Win/7.62mm battle rifle.

The Ruger Mini-14 has been very effective in armed encounters.

The AK rifles have proven superb and were carried by C.I.A. personnel in Afghanistan reportedly when starting the war over there.

The UZI and MP-5 type weapons have proven themselves in protective and anti-terrorist roles.

Heavy barreled, bolt action .308 and .300 Winchester Magnum Precision Rifles by Remington, Winchester, and Steyr have been used by top professionals where distance and precise accuracy are desired.

Benelli and Remington shotguns have been used by U.S. Marines to protect diplomats and for embassy security.

Blackwater tested the Mossberg 930 SPX and thought enough of it to put their name and logo on a version of it.

Winchester 1300 shotguns have been reliable and a good bargain in my experience.

Any of the above firearms should serve you well if you have need of their enhanced capabilities.

Shotguns have the greatest short-range firepower. Years ago, I demonstrated a Benelli M-1 Super 90 with #4 buckshot. More than 200 .24 caliber buckshot pellets destroyed the man-sized target 7 yards away in less than 2 seconds.

Bolt action, heavy barreled precision bolt action rifles are generally the most accurate.

Battle rifles and tactical carbines offer enhanced firepower, good accuracy and extended distance capability.

There is also the intimidation factor. Multiple attackers have been known to think better of it upon seeing a Tactical Rifle.

Recommended long gun ammo

.223/5.56mm

45 to 55gr. J.H.P. or expanding bullets are recommended where over penetration is a concern or for varmint control.

.55gr. M-193 type FMJ ammo is the famed Vietnam era tumbling bullet.

.62gr. Green Tip M-855 type FMJ ammo offers superior penetration on hard targets.

.308Win/7.62mm NATO:

NATO and Military ammo of FMJ type is most commonly used. Soft point ammo can reduce penetration to some degree if desired.

Shotgun:
Good slugs for distance and Buckshot of 00, #1, or #4 type; #6 field loads where over-penetration is a concern.

Final Selection Advice

You have in your hands a guide for making an intelligent and informed decision on the selection of a life saving emergency device.

Armed with this knowledge, make the right choice for you.

Select a quality weapon, inspect your ammo before loading it, learn how to use the gun effectively, and take care of it.

If you do those things, the gun probably will not let you down, when you need it most.

080
Northern Nevada 2014

Epilogue

On the 2nd of August, in the year 1876, Wild Bill Hickock was fatally shot in the back while holding Aces and Eight's, the "Dead Man's Hand". His attacker killed him as a direct result of stealth employment. So was John Westley Hardin, whom many considered to be the greatest gunfighter of all time.

Since that time, many others have died as a result of stealth employment; including Anwar Sadat.

Deadly confrontations are like love affairs, what you don't know can get you killed.

Never turn your back on anything that you have not checked out first… and expect the unexpected.

This book attempts to deal you a winning hand in such matters. I sincerely hope you never need it.

Thank you for your support of my efforts. I wish you and yours a safe pleasant journey through life.

080
The Virginia Highlands,
NV
2014

www.ingramcontent.com/pod-product-compliance
Lightning Source LLC
Chambersburg PA
CBHW040001080526
44586CB00027B/2840